IMAGES
of America

CHICOPEE

IMAGES
of America

CHICOPEE

Michele Plourde-Barker

ARCADIA
PUBLISHING

Copyright © 1998 by Michele Plourde-Barker
ISBN 978-1-5316-6051-2

Published by Arcadia Publishing
Charleston, South Carolina

Library of Congress Catalog Card Number: 98-86557

For all general information contact Arcadia Publishing at:
Telephone 843-853-2070
Fax 843-853-0044
E-mail sales@arcadiapublishing.com
For customer service and orders:
Toll-Free 1-888-313-2665

Visit us on the Internet at www.arcadiapublishing.com

Images of America: Chicopee was written in commemoration of the 150th
anniversary of Chicopee's incorporation as a town.
It is dedicated to the memory of Dr. Daniel I. Hosman and Peter Derosier.

CONTENTS

ACKNOWLEDGMENTS

This project was sponsored by the Chicopee Historical Society and the Edward Bellamy Memorial Association. I would like to thank Molly Hosman and Frank Wotton, the Historical Society's president and vice president, and Society members for their support. Special thanks are due to Steve Jendrysik, president of the Bellamy Association, for providing access to the Bellamy collection, along with work space, supplies, and much-needed encouragement. Thanks also to Michael Baron and his staff at the Chicopee Public Library for the use of the local history collection. And special thanks to Ray Burke, who provided prints from the Joseph Morrow collection and from his own private collection and who graciously made dozens of copy prints for this project. I'd also like to thank the staff of the Chicopee School Department's School-to-Work Program, who shared space, time, and copier privileges with me for the duration. Finally, I would like to acknowledge the following individuals, families, and organizations, who offered images, information, and/or support for the project (and I apologize in advance for any inadvertent omissions).

Maureen Shea Blais, Helen Borak, Jeffrey Sagalyn of Cabotville Industrial Park, John T. Callahan, Reverend Kim E. Stone and members of the Chicopee Falls United Methodist Church, the staff of the Chicopee Planning and Community Development Departments, Gary Tereso and the Chicopee Portuguese Club, Marie and Rick Cienciwa, the Connecticut Valley Historical Museum, the Croteau family, Martha L. Doyle, Yvette Ducharme, Charlie Dugre of the Lucky Strike Restaurant, Raymond Dumont, Elms College librarian Sister Mary Gallagher, First Central Baptist Church historian David Henry, Robert Goyette, Richard Haslam, the Rene Harnisch family, Mr. and Mrs. J. W. Heron, Paul Graves of the Holyoke Public Library, Rena Kantianis, Chet Kobierski, Mayor Richard Kos, Harvey Lafleur, Eric Lalonde, Raymond LaMarche, Mr. and Mrs. Gerard O. LeBlanc, Nellie Leocopoulos, Paul Loranger, the Mason family, the McKinstry family, Maxine M. Metras, Helen Modzelewski, Eileen St. Pierre O'Gorman, Edwin M. Pajak, Joseph Pasternak Jr., Sandra Peret of the Chicopee Visiting Nurses Association, William Phillips, Frank Pieciak, Daniel J. Quirk, Thomas Rockwell and the Normal Rockwell Family Trust, Albert H. Roy, William A. Santos, Frances (Reed) Shaw, Attorney Francis J. Shea, Spalding Sports Worldwide archivist Kathleen Halpin-Robbins, Harriet Supernant, the Fred W. Thomas family, the Warren Tremblay family, Jack Valley, Westover Air Force Base Public Affairs Specialist Monica Lindberg, Jack Woods, and Nick Zades.

INTRODUCTION

Images of America: Chicopee has truly been a citywide effort, with businesses, institutions, and individuals generously coming forward to share their pictures and memories. Well over 30 individuals and organizations contributed images and information for the book, which was sponsored by Chicopee's two historical societies (the Chicopee Historical Society and the Edward Bellamy Memorial Association).

When the Historical Society chose me for this project, I wondered how I would ever find over two hundred photographs to use in this book. Three months and several dozen phone calls later, I found myself wondering how I could choose only two hundred photographs from the nearly one thousand that I had viewed. I learned that tracing a community's history in 225 pictures or less is about like trying to write that history in two thousand words or less. Difficult choices have to be made, and focusing on one subject means that something just as important must inevitably be slighted. It would have been very easy to put together a photo album of random images only connected by the fact that they have something to do with Chicopee. But I wanted each picture or series of pictures to tell the story of the city's growth and the people who made it possible. I wanted this book to be a story book rather than a photo album. I hope I've succeeded.

The story of Chicopee's history was shaped, first of all, by its topography. The city's two rivers attracted farmers and manufacturers. Chicopee's varied landscape—with steep hills, sandy plains, and scattered areas of fertile soil—prevented the city from growing outward around a central core, as many other New England towns did. Instead, the city developed into five separate villages, each with its own distinct identity. Each neighborhood's identity was further refined by the different ethnic groups who came to work in Chicopee's factories and shops. While each neighborhood or ethnic group could easily take up a book of its own, I hope the images in these pages will at least introduce readers to the people and forces that shaped the city.

Because Chicopee has been a manufacturing community for nearly two hundred years, the largest section of the book is devoted to Chicopee's industries. We are fortunate to have a number of photographs that will take readers right into the factories themselves, alongside weavers and spinners, bicycle- and tire-makers, foundrymen and machinists. While no photograph can capture the sound of two thousand looms clattering away, the smell of molten rubber, or the heat of a textile mill on an August afternoon, I hope these images will give readers a better sense of what life might have been like in those old factories.

In 1976, Winthrop McKinstry wrote a history of Chicopee entitled *Glimpses of the Past*. Perhaps that title would be appropriate for this book as well, for photographs do not give us a complete picture of the past, but rather a collection of brief glimpses—moments frozen for us to interpret later at our leisure. In selecting the photographs for this book, I've tried to concentrate on glimpses of everyday life—views that would have been familiar to ordinary Chicopee residents of the 19th and early 20th centuries. For some readers, these glimpses will stir up memories. For others, who are too young to remember Chicopee Falls with its dense network of streets lined with shops and apartment blocks, or Perkins Street's rows of brick tenements, or Johnny cake Hollow's weathered colonial farmhouses, these glimpses will reveal a city they've never seen before. I've placed special emphasis on buildings and streetscapes that no longer exist or that have changed dramatically, so that readers can see what Chicopee looked like before urban renewal and interstate highways altered large sections of the city, and before suburban growth transformed Chicopee's outlying farms into subdivisions and shopping centers.

In 1998, Chicopee celebrates the 150th anniversary of its incorporation as a town, and nearly 350 years of settlement. What better way to celebrate than to take a visual tour through the city's past?

Prologue

FROM FARMS TO
FACTORIES TO TOWN

There is about as much disagreement over the date Chicopee was first settled as there is over the meaning of its name. The word "Chicopee" has been variously interpreted as "birch bark place," "place of the elms," and "turbulent waters." The most reliable translations indicate that the name comes from an Algonquin word for "violent or raging waters."

The Nipmuck Indians were the Algonquin tribe that gave Chicopee its name. The Nipmucks fished the Chicopee and Connecticut Rivers and hunted the area's woodlands before European settlers arrived in the 17th century. Evidence of native occupation has been found in the Chicopee Street and Sandy Hill areas, and near the mouth of the Chicopee River.

In 1636, Englishman William Pynchon led a group of settlers west across Massachusetts from Boston to Springfield. Some sources contend that the first settlement in Chicopee took place two years later, in 1638. However, Pynchon didn't buy Chicopee's land from the Nipmucks until 1641. At first, settlers merely used the northern part of Springfield (the area that would eventually become Chicopee) as pasture for their livestock. It wasn't until 1659 that brothers Henry and Japhet Chapin, Chicopee's first settlers, bought land in Chicopee from John Pynchon. They probably built their homes a few years later.

Sand and gravel soils predominate in Chicopee, except in the Connecticut and Chicopee River floodplains, where early settlers cultivated large tracts of silt-rich topsoil. Farmers concentrated on the Chicopee Street and Chicopee Center areas and on the "Skipmunk" area to the east of Chicopee Falls. For nearly 150 years, Chicopee remained a rural outpost of Springfield. Eventually, however, Chicopee settlers wanted to break from Springfield and establish their own community with their own parishes and local government.

Industrial growth provided the impetus for a final break in the early 19th century, when manufacturers from Boston looked to swiftly running rivers like the Chicopee to power new factories. During the 1820s and 1830s, Chicopee, like Lowell, became one of the state's planned industrial communities, with manufacturers building mills and housing for millworkers on a grand scale. As its industrial sections grew, Chicopee began to see itself as a separate community from Springfield. In 1844, residents began to consider a break from Springfield; in April 1848, the state legislature granted Chicopee its own town charter.

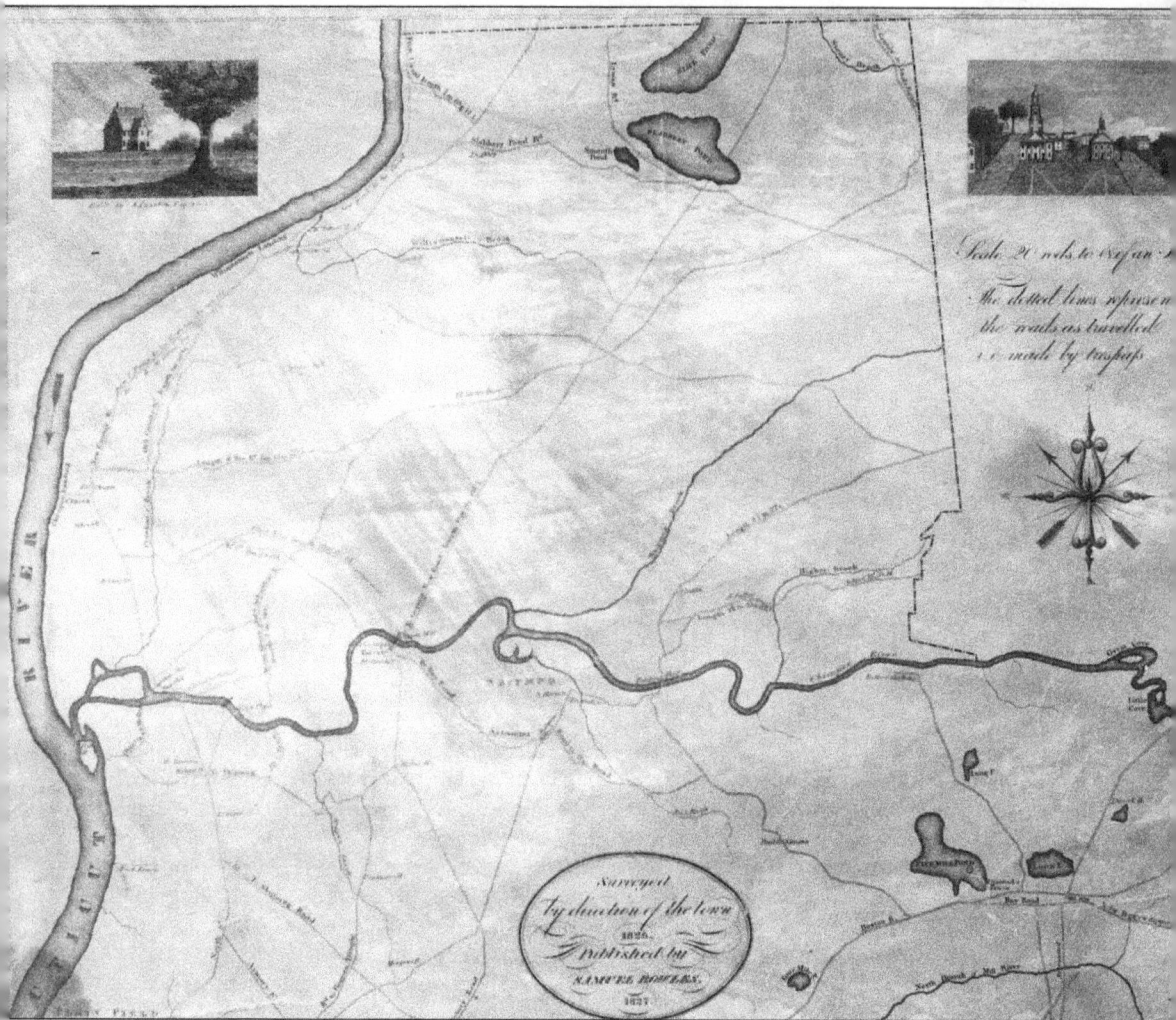

When Samuel Bowles drafted this map of Springfield in 1826, Chicopee was on the verge of becoming a thriving industrial community. Early settlement was concentrated along Chicopee Street and to the east of Chicopee Falls (in the area shown as "Skipmug" on this map). The map shows a few scattered farms, but nothing remotely resembling a town. But Chicopee was already starting to change. Even as Bowles was drawing his map, industrialists were beginning to erect clusters of industrial, residential, and commercial buildings in Chicopee Falls (then known as Factory Village). Within five years, they would begin developing Chicopee Center (known as Cabotville). Within 20 years, Cabotville and Factory Village would be crisscrossed by webs of streets crowded with tenements, boardinghouses, factories, and stores, and the community would be ready to call itself a town. (Courtesy of Connecticut Valley Historical Museum.)

This *c.* 1900 view of the Fuller farm at Bircham Bend shows how Chicopee's landscape might have looked during the 1700s and early 1800s. The site had been cleared and under cultivation fairly early in the area's history, when Chicopee was still primarily an agricultural outpost of Springfield. (George Loomis album; courtesy of Edward Bellamy Memorial Association.)

Chapins were the first settlers to buy land and build homes in Chicopee. Brothers Henry and Japhet Chapin bought large tracts of land in the areas now known as Chicopee Center and Willimansett. Members of the Chapin family were the dominant landowners along Chicopee Street for most of the 1600s and 1700s. The *c.* 1730 Abel Chapin House on Chicopee Street (here shown in a turn-of-the-century postcard view) is one Chapin property that has survived into the 20th century. (Courtesy of Chet Kobierski.)

11

The "Skipmunk" or "Skipmuck" area was settled fairly early in Chicopee's history. Skipmunk boasted rich farmland and provided access to a shallow section of the Chicopee River, where the river could be easily forded. Located west of Chicopee Falls, around the intersection of East Main and Carew Streets, Skipmunk was the site of the Jonathan Cooley House (below) and the Snow House (above). Even at the end of the 19th century, when these photographs were taken, the two sites retained much of their 18th-century appearance. The Snow House (built in the late 1600s) was an especially popular subject for nostalgic drawings and photographs during the 1890s, and was reputed to have housed Chicopee's first Methodist meetings. The Cooley House (built in 1713) was owned by descendants of one of Skipmunk's earliest settlers. The Cooley House burned in 1904. (Top: Courtesy of Edward Bellamy Memorial Association—Bottom: George Loomis album; courtesy of Edward Bellamy Memorial Association.)

For nearly a hundred years, Chicopee's first settlers made the long trek south to Springfield to worship. In 1751, they formed their own parish and built the settlement's First Congregational Church on Chicopee Street. In 1825, the original church was replaced with the building shown at right, which was dedicated in 1826, and is the oldest church building in Chicopee. Although its designer is unknown, it is similar to churches designed by Northampton architect Isaac Damon. (Courtesy of Chet Kobierski.)

Congregationalism dominated religious life in early New England. By the late 1700s and early 1800s, however, other Protestant denominations began to assemble. The Chicopee Falls Methodist Episcopal Church, organized in 1822, was Chicopee's first new congregation. The group first met in homes, schools, and mill buildings before constructing its first church in 1828. The present church (shown below), built in 1841–42, is the oldest religious structure in Chicopee Falls. (Courtesy of Chicopee Falls United Methodist Church.)

The geometric lines of Classical architecture were popular for churches and homes during the first half of the 19th century. Like the churches on the previous page, the First Baptist Church of Chicopee Falls resembled a Greek temple. The First Baptist congregation was organized in 1828 and built its first church in 1832. The church was replaced in 1877 by the present Gothic-style church at the corner of Belcher Street and Broadway. (Lithograph from an ambrotype by E.A. Alden, 1859; courtesy of First Central Baptist Church.)

With the industrial growth of the 1820s and 1830s, some sections of Chicopee began to lose their rural nature. In the heart of Cabotville and Chicopee Falls, views of farmland and woodlots were replaced by vistas of brick industrial, residential, and commercial buildings crowded shoulder-to-shoulder along newly opened streets. This 1839 view of Cabotville shows a bustling town center with massive industrial buildings looming over the river. (Engraving by John Warner Barber, *Historical Collections...*, 1839; courtesy of Frank H. Wotton II.)

One

Two Rivers Run
Through It

Because Chicopee is located at the junction of the Chicopee and the Connecticut Rivers, its history has been closely tied to the two waterways. Before European settlers arrived on the scene, the Nipmucks caught salmon and shad from the banks of the two rivers. English settlers were quick to exploit the rivers' harvest; salmon and shad fisheries were among the area's first commercial ventures.

The wide, deep Connecticut River provided transportation that was more comfortable, convenient, and efficient than overland travel. As settlers cleared Chicopee's forests, they rafted lumber down the Connecticut for sale in Hartford. The river's floodplain provided rich soils for Chicopee's first farms. The advantage of the Chicopee River, on the other hand, lay in its speed and its rapid descent through the landscape's hilly terrain; the river drops over 75 feet between the Chicopee Falls dam and the river's mouth. Settlers initially harnessed the river's turbulent waters to turn waterwheels for gristmills and sawmills to process grain and lumber. Eventually, industrialists found a more profitable use for the swiftly moving river, routing it through canals and raceways to spin the turbines that powered looms, spinning machines, lathes, and other manufacturing equipment, transforming Chicopee from an agricultural village to an industrial town.

While Chicopee's two rivers benefited the city in many ways, they could also be obstacles. Before 1780, Chicopee had no bridges across either river. Travelers crossed the Connecticut River by ferry and the Chicopee River by wading through shallow fords at Cabotville and Skipmunk. By 1850, however, Chicopee boasted not one, but three covered bridges, a railroad trestle, and at least one ferry. The siting of a bridge could promote or hinder a neighborhood's development, and the destruction or abandonment of a bridge could not only reroute travelers, but could also lead to an area's decay.

In 1846, Chicopee residents began lobbying for a bridge across the Connecticut River to West Springfield. In 1848, they got their wish. Construction on the Chicopee-West Springfield bridge began the same year Chicopee declared its independence from Springfield. This 1,237-foot-long covered bridge was engineered by Northampton architect Isaac Damon, using a lattice bridge design developed by Ithiel Towne. Damon specialized in building bridges, churches, and public buildings. Within a three-year time span, Damon built Chicopee's three covered bridges, constructing one at Cabotville and one at Chicopee Falls as well as this one over the Connecticut River. The bridge was privately operated by the Cabot-West Springfield Bridge Company for nearly 25 years before Chicopee, West Springfield, and Hampden County jointly purchased it in 1872. (Top: Courtesy of Edward Bellamy Memorial Association—Bottom: Joseph Morrow Collection; courtesy of Ray Burke.)

In 1903, while the Connecticut River bridge was being repaired, its wooden timbers caught fire. The top photograph, taken just after the fire, shows the smoldering ruins. All that remained were the piers, made of East Longmeadow sandstone. For two years, travelers crossing the Connecticut had to rely on the ferry shown below. (Joseph Morrow Collection; courtesy of Ray Burke.)

In 1905, Springfield's R.F. Hawkins Iron Works built a new bridge on the original bridge's sandstone footings. With the advent of automobile traffic, however, the bridge became too narrow to easily accommodate two lanes of cars. In 1969, after the opening of Interstate 91 created a new highway bridge to West Springfield, the 1905 bridge was abandoned to all but foot traffic. (The photograph at left shows an unidentified hunter crossing from West Springfield to Chicopee in 1972, a few years after the bridge was closed.) After more than 15 years of considering proposals to replace, renovate, or reuse the decaying structure, the city demolished the bridge in 1987–88. The sandstone piers were salvaged and used in renovations at the Smithsonian Institution's Renwick "Castle." (Top: Photograph by Joseph Morrow, 1970s; courtesy of Ray Burke—Left: Photograph by Paul Loranger; Chicopee Historical Society Collection; gift of Paul Loranger.)

The absence of a bridge could hinder the development of an area. For nearly 250 years, travelers could cross from Willimansett to Holyoke only by ferry. While a railroad bridge with a pedestrian walkway was constructed in the 1840s, wagon and horse traffic still had to cross by boat, as shown in the photograph above (*c.* 1880s). After considerable debate about possible bridge sites, construction began on the Willimansett-Holyoke bridge in 1891 (shown below during construction). After the bridge opened in 1893, Willimansett quickly changed from a rural area to a more urban one. Apartment blocks were built to accommodate workers commuting over the bridge to Holyoke factories. Soon Willimansett developed its own commercial and industrial districts. (Top: Courtesy of Chet Kobierski—Bottom: Courtesy of Albert H. Roy.)

This 1879 view of Chicopee Center shows mill buildings clustered on the Chicopee River's banks to take advantage of the rapidly moving water to power their machines. Dams like the one at the center of the photograph helped manufacturers control the flow of water and redirect it into canals and raceways within the mill complexes. (Courtesy of Chet Kobierski.)

In 1783, Chicopee's first covered bridge was constructed at this site. According to local legend, Daniel Shays and his rebels hid on the Chicopee bridge in 1787. The bridge was rebuilt in 1821 (probably into an open bridge as shown in the Barber print on p. 14), and then replaced by this covered bridge in 1846. Isaac Damon, who built the 1848 Chicopee-West Springfield bridge, designed this bridge after the same lattice pattern developed by Ithiel Towne. (Joseph Morrow Collection; courtesy of Ray Burke.)

In 1931, construction began on a new reinforced concrete bridge in Chicopee Center. These two views show the new bridge rising as workers dismantle the old bridge alongside it. In his dedication speech for the new span, Chicopee Mayor Henry Cloutier praised the new structure, while noting that Isaac Damon's old covered bridge was "honor built" and probably could have survived several more years. The new bridge, designed by B.A. Annable and built by Springfield construction firm Fred T. Ley, was completed in a matter of two months. (Courtesy of Edward Bellamy Memorial Association.)

A group of boys stops to take a closer view of the work in progress from a temporary causeway laid across the river during construction of the new bridge. The remnants of the old bridge can be seen collapsing into the river behind the new one. (Courtesy of Edward Bellamy Memorial Association.)

The new bridge was dedicated on November 11, 1931, to great fanfare and a crowd of nearly 25,000 people. The structure was named in honor of Father William F. Davitt, a World War I chaplain from Willimansett who was killed in action just before the Armistice was signed. This photograph was probably taken fairly soon after the bridge was opened. (Courtesy of Spalding Sports Worldwide.)

Chicopee Falls, originally known by its Indian name of "Skenungonuck Falls," is shown here around 1900, in a photograph taken from the north side of the Chicopee River looking southeast. Manufacturers dammed the river at this point to take advantage of the natural drop in the terrain. (Courtesy of Chicopee Falls United Methodist Church.)

Gatehouses, like the one shown in this c. 1921 photograph, controlled the flow of water from the river to Chicopee Falls factories. The gatehouses channeled water into the mills' canals, where it was directed to the turbines that powered manufacturing equipment. (Photograph by Russell Gilbert. Courtesy of Chicopee Public Library.)

When developers began eyeing Chicopee Falls for industrial use in the 1820s, they needed to create more convenient access between the river's north and south banks. The first bridge at the Falls was built in 1821. The covered bridge shown above (in an 1894 photograph) replaced it in 1847. If this bridge looks familiar, that's because it was engineered by Isaac Damon, who designed the 1846 Chicopee Center and 1848 Chicopee-West Springfield bridges. (Hanifan Collection; courtesy of Edward Bellamy Memorial Association.)

For pedestrians wanting a shortcut from their homes on the north side of the Chicopee River to their jobs in the mills (or vice versa—there were factories on both sides of the river at Chicopee Falls), the Fisk Rubber Company constructed a suspension bridge, shown above in an early 20th-century postcard. Built around 1898, the bridge served factory workers until it was washed away in a 1938 flood. (Courtesy of Chet Kobierski.)

In 1905, the Chicopee Falls covered bridge was replaced with an open-decked iron bridge. The new bridge provided separate travel ways for trolleys, vehicular traffic, and pedestrians. In the postcard view above, the three tracks, separated by iron railings, are clearly visible. In the lower view, taken some time between 1923 and 1938, a trolley crosses over to the north side of the river. Because the new bridge accommodated trolley traffic, travelers could now make a continuous journey from Chicopee Falls without having to get off one trolley, cross the old covered bridge on foot, and board a second trolley. (Top: Courtesy of Chet Kobierski—Bottom: Courtesy of Holyoke Public Library.)

Chicopee's proximity to two major rivers has been a mixed blessing. While the rivers have provided transportation, food, and industrial power, they have not always been good neighbors. Historians recorded periodic devastating floods throughout the 19th century. In 1848, the Connecticut River washed away half of the Chicopee-West Springfield bridge, then under construction, and work had to begin anew. In the 20th century, several major floods brought the rivers into the laps of Chicopee residents. In March 1936, a combination of a wet winter and massive spring runoffs caused both rivers to rise beyond their banks. The top picture shows a view of Willimansett covered by the floodwaters. Below, the Davitt Bridge at Chicopee Center barely stayed above the rising water. The city suffered over $3 million in damage from the 1936 flood. (Top: Courtesy of Chicopee Public Library—Bottom: Courtesy of Spalding Sports Worldwide.)

Just two years later, a September hurricane tore through New England. Floodwaters ripped the Chicopee Falls bridge from its footings. The bridge took with it a major water main, leaving parts of the city without water for several days. Pedestrians used the wooden bridge shown below for over a year, until a new bridge was completed in 1940. The new bridge was named for Thomas F. Deady, a Chicopee man killed in WW I. (Hanifan Collection; courtesy of Edward Bellamy Memorial Association.)

The Willimansett area that had been flooded in 1936 suffered a similar inundation in 1938. This view looks down on Chicopee Street from Sandy Hill. The 1936 and 1938 floods led to the construction of a series of dikes along the Connecticut River to keep future floodwaters in check. (Courtesy of Edward Bellamy Memorial Association.)

In August of 1955, an August hurricane again brought the Chicopee River's waters close to the deck of the Davitt Bridge. (Courtesy of Robert Goyette.)

Two

INDUSTRIAE VARIAE

When Chicopee became a town in 1848, its new seal showed the community as a perfect example of 19th-century progress. A railroad engine steams across the lower half of the seal, while brick factory buildings surround it, with their products—armaments, tools, and bales of fabric—stacked in the foreground. Fifty-two years later, when the town became a city, that image of Chicopee as an industrial community hadn't changed; the new city chose *Industriae variae*—"Varied Industries"—as its motto.

While Chicopee had a few manufacturers in the 18th and even 17th centuries, it didn't come into its own as an industrial community until a group of Boston investors decided to create a textile-manufacturing complex based on the Lowell model along the banks of the Chicopee River. They envisioned manufacturing centers at Factory Village (Chicopee Falls) and Cabotville (Chicopee Center) as complete communities, including not only mills, but also tenements and boardinghouses for workers. The first workers were farm girls from Chicopee and surrounding communities, attracted by the opportunity to earn cash wages and by the novelty of a life away from the farm. They were followed by successive waves of immigrant settlers—Irish in the 1830s, French-Canadian in the 1860s, Polish in the 1880s, and finally Greek and Portuguese in the early 20th century.

Through the 19th century, manufacturing prospered, with Chicopee factories turning out textiles, agricultural tools, swords, small arms, and even cannon. By the turn of the 20th century, advances in transportation spurred another industrial boom, with Chicopee factories producing everything from pen clips, chocolates, knitting machines, and boxes, all the way up to bicycles, tires, and automobiles. A discussion of every Chicopee manufacturer would fill a book in itself. The following chapter offers a sampling of Chicopee's historic industries.

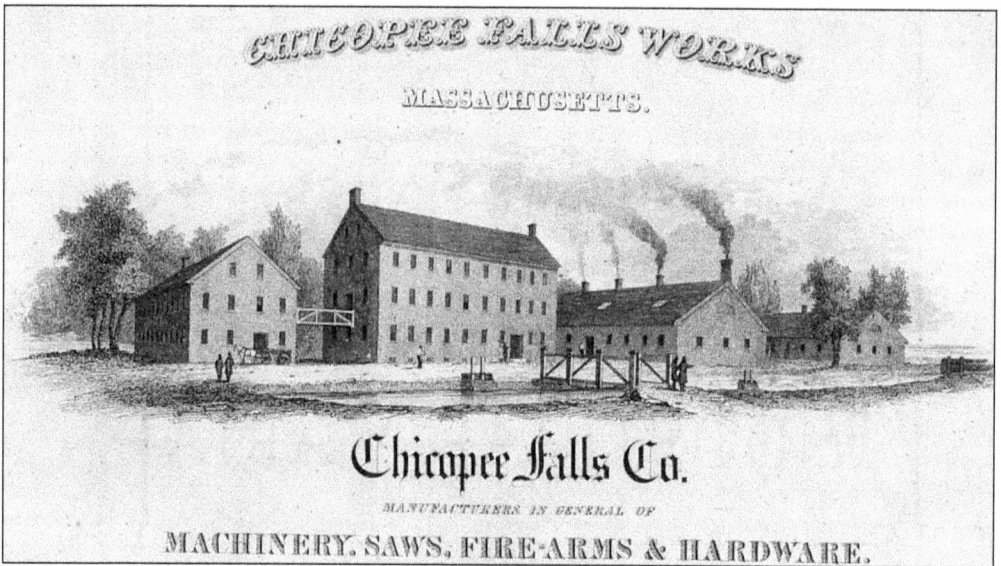

This early advertisement for the Chicopee Falls Company illustrates the appearance and scale of Chicopee's early mill buildings. Established in 1836, the Chicopee Falls Company made saws, hardware, muskets, and some early revolvers. The Ames Manufacturing Company bought out the Chicopee Falls Company in 1841. By 1849, the business had been reorganized as the Massachusetts Arms Company. (Courtesy of Chicopee Public Library.)

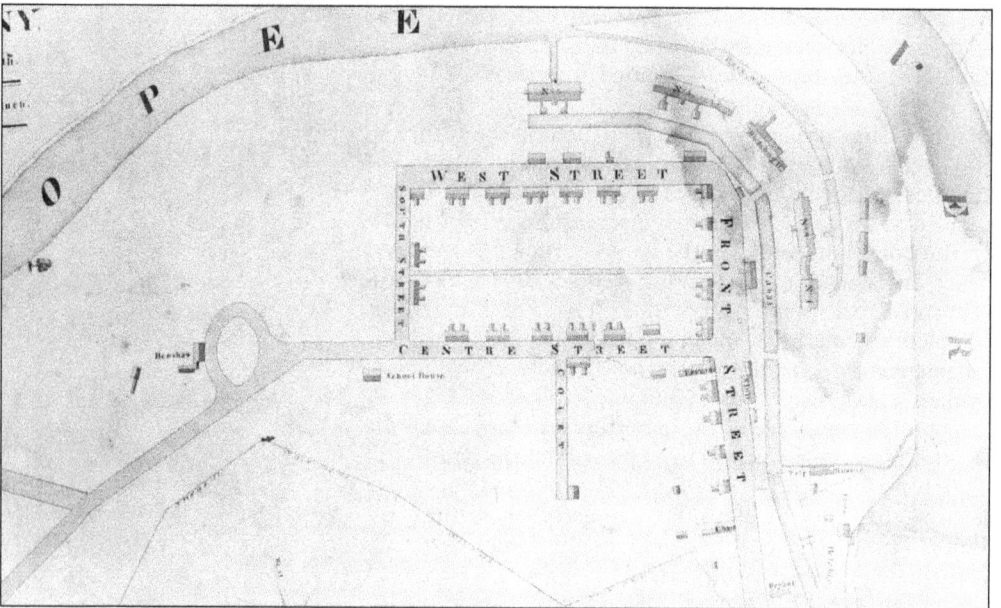

In 1823, Springfield businessman Edmund Dwight and a group of Boston-based investors incorporated the Chicopee Manufacturing Company to create a planned industrial community in Chicopee. In 1825, the company built its first mill in Chicopee Falls. By 1834, when this plan was drawn, the complex included four textile mills, a bleachery, a store, and over two dozen boardinghouses for mill workers. ("Plan of an Estate in Springfield, Belonging to Chickopee Manufacturing Company," by Alex Wadsworth, Boston, Sept. 1834; courtesy of Edward Bellamy Memorial Association.)

The 1857 lithograph above shows the extent of the Chicopee Manufacturing Company's holdings. John Chase, the company's agent, worked with master mason Charles McClallan to construct dams and canals to bring water to the mills. McClallan also built the massive brick industrial buildings and accompanying boarding houses behind, creating an instant town ready for residents and workers. By 1879, the mills had 1,000 operatives manufacturing cotton fabrics. In 1916, not long after the postcard below was printed, the company was taken over by Johnson & Johnson, which operated it until 1975. Then, threatened with the plant's closing, a group of employees bought out the company and incorporated as Facemate Corporation. The company still uses a number of the surviving buildings in its operations. (Top: "Chicopee Falls 1857," lithograph by Endicott & Co., from an ambrotype by A.F. Daniels; courtesy of Edward Bellamy Memorial Association—Bottom: Courtesy of Chet Kobierski.)

31

Another prominent Chicopee Falls manufacturer was the Belcher & Taylor Agricultural Tool Company. Benjamin Belcher established the company as an iron foundry on the south side of Chicopee Falls. Benjamin's sons continued the business, branching out into two different companies, both specializing in agricultural equipment. By the 1890s, the two companies were consolidated as Belcher & Taylor, using facilities on the Chicopee River's north bank (illustrated above). The company kept well abreast of the late 19th-century trend toward mechanized farming. Belcher & Taylor held several patents and promoted its products (like the "National Rake" in the ad below) as the scientific solution to the modern farmer's needs. The company continued its operations in Chicopee until 1923, when an outside producer bought Belcher & Taylor and closed the Chicopee plant. (Top: Illustration from G.H.T. Babbitt, *Chicopee Falls Past and Present*, 1893; courtesy of Edward Bellamy Memorial Association— Bottom: Courtesy of Chet Kobierski.)

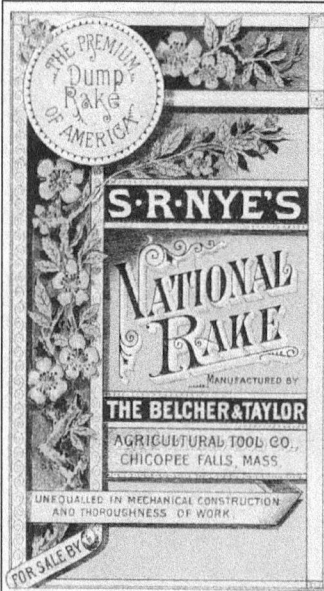

The Industrial Revolution brought mechanization even to such homey activities as knitting. In 1867, the Lamb Knitting Machine Company was formed to manufacture a revolutionary knitting machine, which could make any stitches a human knitter could. Various models of the Lamb machine were marketed both to home knitters and to manufacturers. Later, the company branched out into the manufacture of eggbeaters, bicycles, and even firearms. The company underwent several reorganizations through its history, suffering a major setback during the Depression; however, unlike many other businesses, it managed to survive through the 1930s. In 1942, Lamb relocated its plant to the north side of the river. In the 1970s, the company moved out to New Lombard Road, where it remains today. The engraving above shows the Lamb factory in the late 19th century. The photograph below shows a 1935 view of the factory near the Chicopee Falls bridge. (Top: Courtesy of Chet Kobierski—Bottom: Courtesy of Holyoke Public Library.)

The 19th century saw many innovations in transportation, from railroads to steamships to trolleys to bicycles to automobiles. Chicopee manufacturers capitalized on these inventions—most notably the bicycle and the automobile. In the 1880s, Albert C. Overman took advantage of the bicycle craze by contracting with the Ames Manufacturing Company to make the new contraptions. Within ten years, sales of Overman's Victor bicycle had increased so much that Overman built a factory on Walnut Street in Chicopee Falls. The Overman Wheel Company's new plant was considered such a fine example of a modern factory that it made the front page of *Scientific American*, from which these illustrations are taken. The article noted that Overman's buildings were built with the most modern fireproof construction, that the plant was centrally heated and fully electrified, and that "the machinery employed in doing the work is the best that money can purchase or that genius can devise." (*Scientific American*, May 2, 1891; courtesy of Chet Kobierski.)

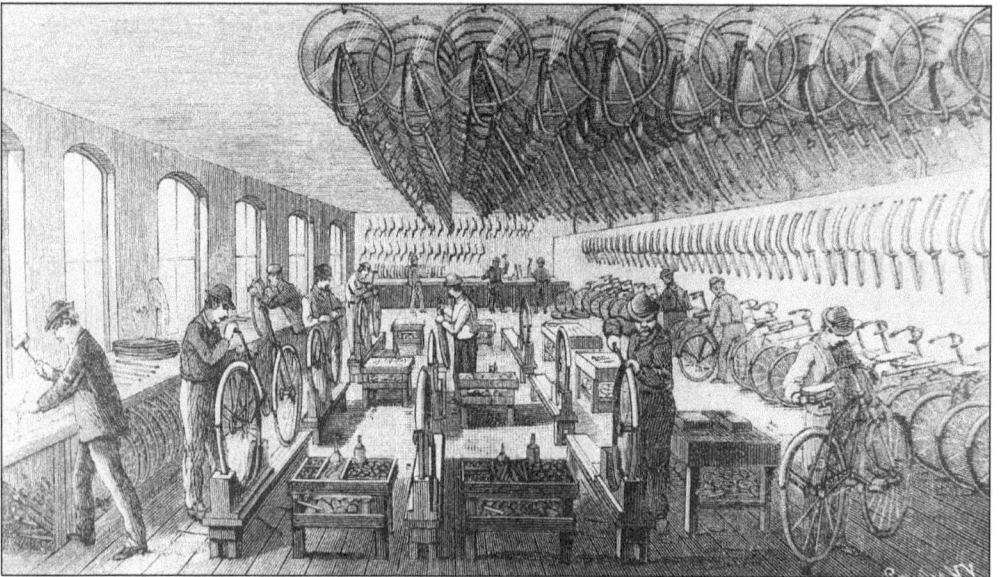

The photograph above, taken in the 1890s, shows Overman workers assembling frames for the famous Victor bicycle. During the peak of production, Overman cultivated a staff of highly skilled workers. Overman boasted that his company used no contract labor or child labor. Overman marketed his products aggressively, and became well known for eye-catching advertisements like the one at left. For a while, sporting-goods manufacturer A.G. Spalding acted as a sales agent for the Victor bicycle, giving Overman an even wider market. Spalding soon began making his own bicycle, and became one of Overman's main competitors. The bicycle industry overestimated its market, however; by the turn of the century, bicycle sales overall had begun to collapse. Overman made a few attempts to get into the new automobile industry, but failed. The plant was eventually sold to the Stevens Arms and Tool Company. (Top: Joseph Morrow Collection; courtesy of Ray Burke— Bottom: Courtesy of Chet Kobierski.)

After closing, the Overman Wheel Company factory was quickly bought by Stevens Arms and Tool Company. Stevens had a long history in Chicopee Falls. In 1849 Joshua Stevens, who had worked for Colt in Connecticut, moved to Chicopee to work at the Massachusetts Arms Company. Stevens had initiated many improvements in revolver design for both Colt and Massachusetts Arms. By 1864, he was ready to strike out on his own. He set up a small shop making arms and mechanics' tools. In 1885, he formally incorporated as the J. Stevens Arms and Tool Company. When Overman folded, Stevens was ready to buy the plant to expand his production facilities. The view above shows the plant under its new management. Below is a view inside one of the shops, probably some time between 1905 and 1915. One of the boys at the center is Patrick J. Hanifan, who worked at Stevens from 1904 until 1931. (Top: Photograph by R.F. Dillingham; courtesy of Chet Kobierski—Bottom: Courtesy of Edward Bellamy Memorial Association.)

In the photograph above, a group of fierce-looking Stevens workers pose with a few samples of their products. Many manufacturers sponsored clubs, bands, and athletic teams for their workers. Stevens was no exception. Below, the Stevens Band of 1907 has apparently just won a musical competition. The bandleader is Major Edward Henry Elder. (Top: Courtesy of Edward Bellamy Memorial Association—Bottom: Courtesy of Chet Kobierski.)

In 1916, Westinghouse took over Stevens Arms. In 1920, Stevens merged with Savage Arms, which continued manufacturing in Chicopee Falls until 1960, when the company moved to Westfield. For many years, the company ran two plants—one on the southern bank of the Chicopee River (the "river plant"), and another at the old Overman Wheel Company factory (the "hill plant"). During both World Wars, government contracts kept the company busy. The photo above shows Savage Arms workers assembled at a 1943 war rally to receive an Army-Navy "E for Excellence" award. When he founded his company, Joshua Stevens supplemented the manufacture of armaments with the manufacture of mechanics' tools as a form of insurance against times when firearms sales were down. Savage Arms continued this policy, branching off into the production of lawn mowers. In the c. 1950s photo at left, workers assemble lawn mowers at Savage's hill plant. (Top: Courtesy of Jack Woods—Left: Courtesy of collection of John Callahan.)

The Stevens company was not only an innovator in the field of armaments; it also branched out to the production of automobiles. The actual site of the invention of the Duryea automobile, America's first gasoline-powered vehicle, is a point of contention between the cities of Springfield and Chicopee. Brothers Frank and Charles Duryea lived in both cities around the time they developed the car in the early 1890s; hence, each community claims to have given birth to the invention. To further muddy the waters, the Duryea brothers (and their descendants) feuded over which brother had actually invented the machine. At any rate, Frank Duryea enlisted the Stevens machine shops in the construction of the car. By 1902, the company was manufacturing the Stevens-Duryea car along the banks of the Chicopee River, in the Chicopee Falls facility shown in these two views. (Courtesy of Chet Kobierski.)

Rows of Stevens-Duryea cars stand ready for testing in the 1905 photograph above. At the left, from front to rear, are testers Clark, Brevier, Stafford, Y[oung?], Carlton, Flynn, Hebert, Strong, Galbraith, Marr, Shaw, Raycroft, Smith, Burlingame, Davis, and St. Martin, ready to drive the Model S six-cylinder car, which boasted 65 horsepower and sold for $6,500. At the right, from front to rear, testers St. Marie, (the next two drivers are unidentified), Bellerose, Gilhooly, Barton, Bozakis, and Tanner prepare to test the Model L, which must have been the budget model. The L was a four-cylinder, 18-horsepower car selling for $2,500. Below, Dr. Michael Shea takes his nephew Cyril E. Shea out for a spin down Belcher Street in his new Stevens-Duryea. Stevens-Duryea's life in Chicopee was brief. By 1922, unable to compete with Midwestern manufacturers, the company had folded. (Top: Joseph Morrow Collection; courtesy of Ray Burke—Bottom: Courtesy of Maureen Shea Blais.)

Another transportation-related company that prospered in Chicopee was the Fisk Rubber Company. In 1896, the Spaulding & Pepper Rubber Company was organized to make bicycle tires. The fledgling company failed and was bought by Noyes W. Fisk, who continued making bicycle tires. When the bicycle market declined, Fisk turned to the new automotive industry for business. By 1904, most of the country's major car manufacturers were buying Fisk tires. By 1912, the rubber company employed more workers than all of the city's cotton manufacturers combined. The view above shows the Fisk company's early facilities. The postcard below shows the extent to which the company had expanded by 1930. The Classical-style business office on Grove Street in Chicopee Falls (the building to the far left, built in 1915–16) still stands, as do many of the industrial buildings at the rear. (Courtesy of Chet Kobierski.)

The Red Top tire, one of Fisk's trademark products, takes center stage on a Fisk parade float from the early 20th century. In the 1919 photograph below, Fisk workers pull apart a block of rubber to prepare it for processing. By 1930, Fisk employed four thousand laborers. (Top: Chicopee Historical Society Collection; gift of Daniel J. Quirk—Bottom: Courtesy of William A. Santos.)

During the 1910s and 1920s, about 10 to 15 percent of Fisk workers were women. In the 1919 photograph above, over a dozen young women attach valve stems to tires. In the photograph below, taken in the early 1920s, Fisk workers display nearly completed tires. During WW I, the Fisk Rubber Company became the city's largest employer. (Top: Courtesy of William A. Santos— Bottom: Chicopee Historical Society Collection; gift of the Fred W. Thomas Family.)

Like most of Chicopee's major industries, Fisk drew many of its workers from the immigrants who had recently moved to the city. The safety bulletin shown in the 1919 photograph at left offers warnings in both English and Polish. If a worker didn't heed the safety advice, Fisk had its own medical staff to treat some injuries in the factory's infirmary, shown in the 1919 photograph below. (Courtesy of William A. Santos.)

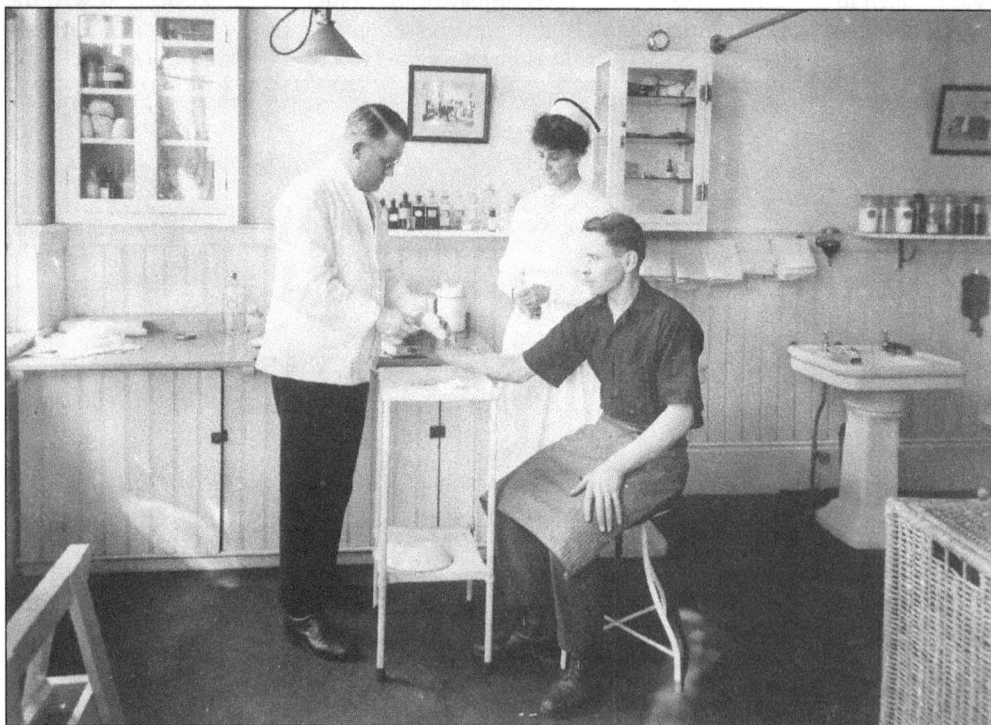

In this 1919 photograph, Fisk's fleet of trucks is being loaded and dispatched. Fisk quickly developed an international as well as a national market. (Courtesy of William A. Santos.)

During the early 20th century, Fisk's yawning "Time to Re-Tire" boy became almost as ubiquitous as today's Energizer bunny. Burr E. Giffen, an 18-year-old Fisk advertising department artist, created the trademark in 1907. Fisk hired some of America's most prominent commercial artists, including Maxfield Parrish and Norman Rockwell, to design the company's ads. Rockwell created this "Sleeping Sheriff" ad for Fisk in 1924. (From the collection of Chet Kobierski; courtesy of the Normal Rockwell Family Trust.)

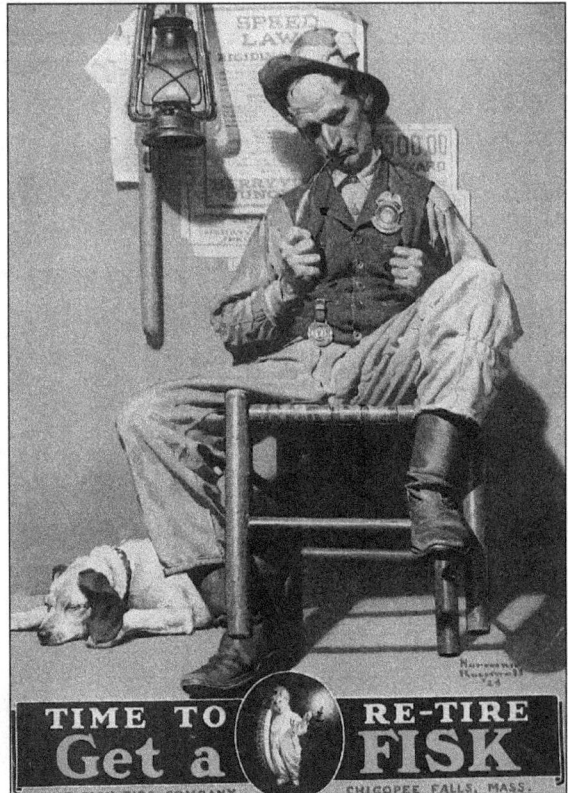

TIME TO Get a RE-TIRE FISK

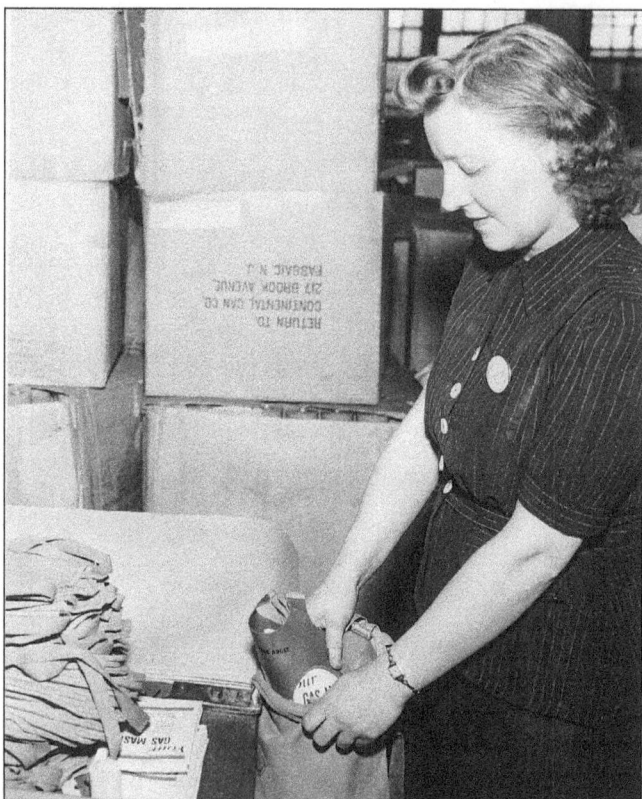

In spite of its successes during the 1910s and 1920s, Fisk suffered a major setback during the Depression, and was forced to close for a short time. The company was reorganized, then became a subsidiary of the United States Rubber Company (now known as Uniroyal) in 1939. Under the new business arrangement, the plant recovered and expanded. During WW II, U.S. Rubber secured a number of government contracts. In the photograph at left, a worker packs gas masks for shipment. In the view below, workers assemble fuel tanks for long-range aircraft. The company remained a major employer in Chicopee until the parent company closed the Chicopee facility in 1981. (Chicopee Historical Society Collection; gift of Daniel J. Quirk.)

While Chicopee Falls was developing as an industrial center, Cabotville, just downstream, was experiencing a parallel surge in growth. In 1825, the Chicopee Manufacturing Company bought land and water rights at Cabotville, and in 1831 organized the Springfield Canal Company to develop that property. John Chase and Charles McClallan oversaw the construction of the new industrial complex. Three separate companies first operated the mills—the Cabot Manufacturing Company, the Perkins Manufacturing Company, and the Dwight Manufacturing Company. In 1856 the three merged under the Dwight name. The view above shows the Dwight mills in 1856. The *c.* 1900 photograph below shows the inside of the complex, looking along the canal. (Top: "Chicopee, Massachusetts, 1856," lithograph of Endicott & Co., from an ambrotype by Spooner Brothers; Chicopee Historical Society Collection; gift of Martha L. Doyle and Maxine M. Metras—Bottom: Allen/Kerr Collection; courtesy of Edward Bellamy Memorial Association.)

Because there were few workers available in the immediate area, the mills at Chicopee Falls and Cabotville had to attract employees from surrounding towns. The first mill workers were primarily young rural women who wanted to earn money to save for marriage, finance their educations, or pay their families' debts. Since there was no housing readily available near the new mills, manufacturers built large company-run boardinghouses like those on Perkins Street (above). These boardinghouses provided well-supervised accommodations for the girls, whose lives were closely regulated. The next level of workers—machinists, overseers, and skilled workers—lived in smaller single- or two-family houses built by the company and sold to private owners. Many of these became private boardinghouses like the one shown below, located on the corner of Cabot and Dwight Streets. This photograph shows "Mother Cole's Boardinghouse" and its tenants around 1860. (Courtesy of Chicopee Public Library.)

The Dwight Manufacturing Company continued to expand through the 19th century. This 1900 plan shows the extensive manufacturing and housing complex created by the company. By 1915, the eight waterwheels powering the mills had been supplemented by three electrical engines to supply power when water levels became low. (Courtesy of Cabotville Industrial Park.)

At the Dwight mills, girls and young women tended to be employed as mill operatives (running the looms and other machines that made thread, yarn, and cloth), while men tended to work as overseers and machinists (supervising the operatives' work and maintaining and repairing machinery). Manufacturers like Dwight distributed promotional brochures encouraging whole families to come work in the mills. Children twelve or younger, like some of the boys and girls in this c. 1910s photograph of Dwight mill hands, were frequently employed in the textile mills. (Courtesy of Edward Bellamy Memorial Association.)

A 1915 Dwight Manufacturing Company promotional brochure enticed workers with promises of comfortable housing, medical services, and other amenities that were either provided by the company or available as city services. Chicopee's schools, parks, roads, and churches seemed to be a major selling point. The brochure also promised workers that they would use the safest and most modern equipment, including automatic Draper looms "of the latest designs." Draper also manufactured the warping machine shown in the photograph above. In the warping process, workers arranged the warp (vertical) threads into the proper order prior to setting them on the loom for weaving. By modern standards, Dwight's workers spent a long day at their machines. Early mill hands often worked for 12 to 14 hours. By the 1910s, when the picture above was taken, the workday had been reduced to 10 hours, with a half day on Saturday. In the c. 1920s photo at left, a young woman takes a short break from tending her spinning machine. (Top: Courtesy of Edward Bellamy Memorial Association—Left: Courtesy of Chicopee Historical Society.)

In 1927, the Dwight Manufacturing Company relocated to Alabama, closing its Chicopee plant. This photo of mill workers was taken shortly before the mill closed. The Depression followed close on the heels of the Dwight mill closing. The Industrial Buildings Corporation was formed in 1929 in order to sell the complex, but was unsuccessful. The second woman from the left in the first row is Catherine Pasternak (kneeling). The fourth woman from the left in the next-to-the-last row is Mary Korona. (Courtesy of Joseph Pasternak Jr.)

In 1932, Raphael Sagalyn bought the Dwight mill complex and managed the Industrial Buildings Corporation as an industrial park and small-business incubator. The photograph at right shows IBC workers during the 1940s. From left to right they are as follows: (front row) all remain unidentified; (second row) two unidentified men, Mr. Pytko, Pete Peterson, and Mr. Trela; (third row) two unidentified men, Pete Cartelli, and W. Konicki; (fourth row) an unidentified man, Mr. Torkington, and three unidentified men; (back row, in suits) Archie Burak and Julian Sagalyn. (Courtesy of Chet Kobierski.)

In 1791, Nathan P. Ames Sr. formed a company to manufacture edge tools in Chelmsford, Massachusetts. In 1829, Nathan Ames Jr. relocated to Chicopee to set up a factory to make swords for the government. He built his first plant (shown in the print above) at Chicopee Falls. By 1834, Ames had moved his factory to Cabotville, and soon expanded his line to include cannon, manufacturing equipment, and bronze castings. The photo below, taken in the 1850s, shows Ames workers posing in the center of Market Square. They are holding up a plaque or a platter—perhaps a product of the company's bronze casting foundry. (Top: Szetela Collection; courtesy of Edward Bellamy Memorial Association—Bottom: Courtesy of Connecticut Valley Historical Museum.)

The Ames company prospered during the Civil War, making swords, bayonets, and cannon. The print above shows part of the manufacturing plant during the 1860s. The Ames factory was located on the other side of the Chicopee River bridge from the Dwight Manufacturing Company. Ames and Dwight dominated Cabotville's industrial scene through the 19th century. (Szetela Collection; courtesy of Edward Bellamy Memorial Association.)

In 1880, the Ames Manufacturing Company split its sword-making operation into a separate division from the main company. The photograph above, taken in 1898, shows Ames Sword Company workers pouring molten metal into molds in the factory's casting foundry. (Szetela Collection; courtesy of Edward Bellamy Memorial Association.)

53

The Ames Sword Company also specialized in making ceremonial regalia for military and fraternal organizations. In the photograph above, taken in 1898, women make uniform hats in the company's sewing shop. The photograph below shows a display of the Ames Sword Company's products. During the 1890s, the main plant of the Ames Manufacturing Company was turned over to the manufacture of bicycles for the Overman Wheel Company. When Overman opened its own facilities in Chicopee Falls, the Ames Manufacturing Company folded, leaving only the Ames Sword Company in operation. Most of the Ames buildings were purchased by A.G. Spalding & Bros., makers of sporting goods. The Ames Sword Company division continued in operation until 1930. In 1935, part of the Ames complex was razed. (Szetela Collection; courtesy of Edward Bellamy Memorial Association.)

Under the direction of Silas Mosman Jr., the Ames Manufacturing Company's bronze foundry, established in 1853, became nationally known for its finely crafted statues and memorials. Mosman's most famous commission was the casting of the doors for the east wing of the Capitol building in Washington, D.C. Designed by Thomas Crawford and William Rinehart in 1853, the doors were fabricated by Mosman in 1867–68. Shown at right, the doors depict a number of Revolutionary War scenes. Mosman and his crew are shown in the photograph above, which was taken in 1868. Silas is the bearded man sitting in the center of the group; his son Melzar stands on the far left. The man to the left of Silas is Edward Buttrick; the man on the far right is a Mr. Joslyn. The other workers are unidentified. (Top: Allen/Kerr Collection; courtesy of Edward Bellamy Memorial Association— Bottom: Szetela Collection; courtesy of Edward Bellamy Memorial Association.)

Silas Mosman's son Melzar also began his career in the Ames shops, but he traveled abroad to improve his knowledge of casting and sculpture. In 1884, he set up his own foundry on Gilmore Street. In 1903-1905, Melzar cast the doors to the Capitol building's west wing. A sculptor as well as a founder, Melzar earned a national reputation for the many war memorials he designed and cast, including this 1921 memorial on Front Street in Chicopee. (Szetela Collection; courtesy of Edward Bellamy Memorial Association.)

Another manufacturer who started out at Ames was Emerson Gaylord, who worked in the Ames leather shop. In 1856, Gaylord bought the leather division and founded the Gaylord Manufacturing Company. The company prospered, making locks and ceremonial swords as well as leather goods. Gaylord's factory operated in these buildings in the Ames complex. In 1881, Gaylord sold his company to the Ames Sword Company. (Allen/Kerr Collection; courtesy of Edward Bellamy Memorial Association.)

56

In the 1890s, Chicago-based sporting-goods manufacturer A.G. Spalding began cashing in on the bicycle craze, selling Victor bicycles for the Overman Wheel Company. Spalding's company soon began making its own bicycles, contracting with the Lamb Company in Chicopee Falls. In 1901, Spalding relocated its entire manufacturing plant to Chicopee. When the bottom fell out of the bicycle market, Spalding was manufacturing such a wide range of other sporting goods that the company managed to survive. By 1904, Spalding was so successful that it expanded into the abandoned Ames factory complex. The view above shows the complex from the Chicopee River. The photograph below, taken in the 1940s, shows the plant just before it relocated away from Chicopee Center. In the 1980s, the old Spalding plant at Chicopee Center was renovated for housing. (Top: Courtesy of Edward Bellamy Memorial Association—Bottom: Courtesy of Spalding Sports Worldwide.)

The photograph above shows Spalding workers at the old Ames complex in the 1920s or 1930s. (The man in the second row on the far right is identified as Albert Meyer, who was employed as a woodworker at Spalding.) In 1948, the company bought the old fairgrounds on Meadow Street in Willimansett to build its new manufacturing plant (shown below fairly soon after opening). The new facilities (still occupied by Spalding today) featured a complete rubber factory, machine shops, woodworking shops, a leather factory, a metalworking factory, and a six-bed hospital. (Top: Courtesy of Edward Bellamy Memorial Association—Bottom: Courtesy of Spalding Sports Worldwide.)

The company's founder, A.G. Spalding, began his career as a professional baseball player, pitching for the Boston Red Stockings in the 1870s. Spalding developed his own baseball design, which became the first officially accepted Major League ball in 1876. Spalding quickly expanded his product line to embrace other sports. The Spalding Company boasted many "firsts" in the field of sports equipment. In 1887, the company produced the first American-made footballs. When James Naismith invented basketball, Spalding became the first company to manufacture equipment for the new sport. In 1888, Spalding became the first American company to manufacture tennis equipment. In the photograph above (taken in the late 1940s), tennis racket frames wait to be strung. While Spalding expanded its product line to embrace a variety of sports, baseball equipment remained one of its mainstays. Below, Spalding workers in the Willimansett plant pack baseballs. (Courtesy of Spalding Sports Worldwide.)

Spalding was also a leader in the manufacture of golf equipment. In 1895, the company became the first U.S. producer of golf balls. Over the next hundred years, the company introduced a number of innovations in the manufacture of balls and clubs for the sport. In the photograph at left, from the late 1940s, metal polisher Bill St. Pierre buffs iron golf club heads. (Courtesy of Eileen St. Pierre O'Gorman.)

In 1948, Spalding workers celebrated Chicopee's 100th anniversary as a town. Seated on the ground are Fran Buckley (at far left), Willard Stratton (second from left), and Bernie Lafleur (fifth from left). On the float, from left to right are Stanley Tatara as a 19th-century baseball player, Roger Sampson as modern ballplayer, Therese Beauchemin, Alice Daigle, Jean Messier, Teresa House, Francis Gula, and Doris Laverty. The woman in the hat and dark coat is Leona Glowski. (Courtesy of Spalding Sports Worldwide.)

Dozens of small manufacturing operations existed alongside the large manufacturers described in the preceding pages. The Burtworth Carpet Company, located on Front Street near the present Electric Light Department offices, operated in Chicopee from 1893 to 1932. In this photograph, taken between 1904 and 1916, weaver Albert Meyer tends a loom. (Courtesy of Edward Bellamy Memorial Association.)

Not all of Chicopee's manufacturers occupied massive brick industrial buildings. One of Chicopee's early industries had a rather unimpressive home here on the corner of Chicopee Street and McKinstry Avenue. In 1836, Daniel Monroe Chapin and Alonzo Phillips made the country's first friction matches, using this house's ell and a small brick building in the backyard. At its peak, the company employed fewer than 25 workers. (Courtesy of Albert H. Roy.)

Travelers going from Holyoke to Chicopee across the Willimansett Bridge saw this impressive view of the Hampden Brewing Company, founded in 1894. During Prohibition, the brewery survived by making malt syrup for export to Canada. After Prohibition ended, the brewery expanded, building a large addition in 1935. In 1963, the Hampden Brewery bought out the New York-based Piels Brothers Brewery, and continued brewing under the Piels name until 1975. (Courtesy of Holyoke Public Library.)

Willimansett's industries were more scattered than those of Chicopee Falls and Cabotville, and developed later. With the construction of trolley lines and, later, the use of automobiles, Willimansett began to attract new industries. Small companies like the L.C. Van Valkenburg Company (shown here in a c. 1921 photograph), began to spring up along Willimansett's railroad lines and its major trolley and automobile routes. Van Valkenburg was founded in 1896 to manufacture small metal products like pen and pencil clips, hair curlers, and fountain pen tips. (Photograph by Russell Gilbert; courtesy of Chicopee Public Library.)

Three

FROM TOWN TO CITY

At first, Chicopee's manufacturers provided many of the public improvements now considered the responsibility of a municipal government. They didn't have much choice; when Chicopee was still a part of Springfield, the parent community made little effort to extend services to outlying areas, partly because the town didn't have the money, and partly because Chicopee was too sparsely settled to justify the expense. The industrialists who created the new mills and accompanying housing created a problem as well: who would provide services for all the workers that the mills were going to attract to Cabotville and Chicopee Falls, never mind the families of those workers? At first, the mill owners were the only ones with the capital to provide amenities such as schools, libraries, parks, fire protection, road improvements, and utilities. Acting on the premise that good public services would attract merchants and new investors as well as workers, Chicopee's early manufacturers contributed large sums toward the creation of public improvements.

As Chicopee grew and developed a tax base of its own, the community assumed more and more responsibility for public improvements. Through the 19th century, the concept of municipal responsibility evolved from the idea that a town or city government should only provide necessities, such as roads and schools and fire protection, to the idea that municipal government was supposed to uplift its citizens, providing a community that not only functioned efficiently, but was pleasant and attractive to live in.

By 1890, Chicopee's population had grown to 14,050—large enough to qualify for a city charter. The charter was granted, and the town began to look at itself in a different light.

For the first 20 years of its existence as an independent town, Chicopee didn't even have a town hall. Meetings were held in Cabot Hall on the corner of Exchange Street and Market Square (not to be confused with the Cabot House in Market Square). In addition to providing town meeting space, Cabot Hall (shown here in the 1890s) hosted lectures by visiting celebrities such as author Charles Dickens and actor Edwin Booth. In the 1890s, Cabot Hall became the Wells Opera House. (Szetela Collection; courtesy of Edward Bellamy Memorial Association.)

In 1870, Chicopee finally got its own town hall, designed by architect Charles G. Parker. With its cantilevered tower, this High Victorian Gothic building dominates Market Square. Supposedly modeled after Florence's Palazzo Vecchio, the hall's design was somewhat unusual for Chicopee at the time. A few years after the hall was completed, historian Louis Everts described its "lofty tower" as having a "peculiar form, but with possible Oriental precedents." (Courtesy of David Henry.)

The city hall auditorium (shown above decorated for a 1914 charity ball) was as elegant as the building's exterior. In 1879, historian Louis Everts described the hall as "handsomely frescoed, with stained-glass windows, and a seating capacity for nine hundred persons." Public meetings, high school graduations, parties, band concerts, theatrical performances, balls, and lectures were held in the auditorium. In the photograph below, taken in 1915, a group of city hall staff celebrates the 25th anniversary of the city's charter. The second man from the right in the back row is probably Mayor Frank A. Rivers. (Top: Courtesy of Chicopee Public Library—Bottom: Joseph Morrow Collection; courtesy of Edward Bellamy Memorial Association.)

In 1846, the Cabot Institute, a private literary club, was established as Chicopee's first library. In 1853, the Institute turned its collection over to the town to establish a public library. Use of the library at first cost patrons 50¢ a year. When the new town hall was built in 1871, the library was given a room for its collection. In 20 years, the library outgrew its quarters, and moved into the old Jerome Wells House on Market Square next to city hall. The brick double house shown above served as the library until 1913. Merchant Justin Spaulding willed $20,000 to the city for the construction of a new library. Additional funds were donated by businessmen N.P. Ames Carter, James L. Pease, and Emerson Gaylord. On May 31, 1913, the new library was dedicated. The library (shown below in a c. 1915 photograph) was designed by the Springfield architectural firm of Kirkham and Parlett, who also designed Springfield's Forbes & Wallace building. (Top: Courtesy of Chet Kobierski—Bottom: Courtesy of Chicopee Public Library.)

In 1879, historian Louis Everts wrote that "a crowning glory of this village is its excellent schools, in which the various grades are ably taught." Because Springfield's schools were nearly inaccessible to Chicopee residents, Chicopee began building its own schools in the early 18th century. At Chicopee Center, Grape Street once had no fewer than three schools. This schoolhouse was built on the corner of Grape and Auburn Streets in 1861. (Photograph by Russell Gilbert, *c.* 1921; courtesy of Chicopee Public Library.)

With four classrooms, the Spruce Street School (built on Cabotville Common in 1849) was fairly large for its time. It became an important resource for Cabotville's French-Canadian and Polish immigrants during the 1890s. Evening school sessions were packed with as many as 195 pupils eager to learn English and other subjects. The school was closed in 1955 and demolished in 1965 to create space for a wading pool. (Photograph by Russell Gilbert, *c.* 1921; courtesy of Chicopee Public Library.)

On the left, the Robinson School (originally the Grape Street School) was built in 1842 as Chicopee Center's first high school. It was renamed in honor of George D. Robinson, principal of the school from 1865 to 1866. Robinson became a prominent lawyer and went on to become governor of Massachusetts. To the right, Valentine School (named after Grape Street Grammar School principal William Valentine) was added to the site in 1899. (Courtesy of Chet Kobierski.)

School Street had its first school in 1834. The stylish Victorian Gothic building shown above replaced the original building in 1876. It served as a school until the 1930s. From 1944 to 1967, the building was used as office space for the Municipal Welfare Department and the Veterans' Services Department. In 1979, the building was demolished. The site is now a parking lot. (Photograph by Russell Gilbert, c. 1921; courtesy of Chicopee Public Library.)

Chicopee Falls had its own schoolhouse at Skipmunk as early as 1812. As the Falls industrial center grew, the city began building schools closer to the mills. The 1870 Sheridan Street School (above), named after Civil War General Philip H. Sheridan, replaced an earlier school in the Falls. The Sheridan Street School was demolished in 1963. (Photograph by Russell Gilbert, c. 1921; courtesy of Chicopee Public Library.)

The Boston and Springfield Manufacturing Company was one of many manufacturers who helped build Chicopee schools. In 1825, the company built the city's first high school on Church Street in Chicopee Falls. The original school was replaced in 1845 by the brick Italianate building shown above, which served as the Chicopee Falls high school until 1890, when the city's Central High School opened. During WW II, the building served as Chicopee's USO headquarters. (Courtesy of Chicopee Public Library.)

This Victorian schoolhouse was built on Broadway in 1875–76. When the Overman Wheel Company built its factory next door, local historian L.L. Johnson wrote that the noise from "the manufacture of bicycles...so interferes with the progress of education...that the teachers wish either that they had never been born, or that the bicycle had never been invented." In 1893, Overman solved the problem by buying the schoolhouse, which then became a factory. (Szetela Collection; courtesy of Edward Bellamy Memorial Association.)

The George S. Taylor School was named after Chicopee's first mayor, an industrialist and partner in the firm of Belcher & Taylor. Taylor held a number of other city offices and served as a state representative and senator. Taylor School was built on Belcher Street in Chicopee Falls in 1910, and once housed the Chicopee Falls Branch Library. The school was demolished in 1970 as a part of the Chicopee Falls urban renewal program. (Photograph by Joseph Morrow. Courtesy of Ray Burke.)

Chicopee built a number of suburban schools in Willimansett, Fairview, and Aldenville. Some were substantial brick buildings. Others, like the North Chicopee School shown above, were more modest. This one-room wooden schoolhouse was used from 1904 until 1947. (Photograph by Russell Gilbert, c. 1921; courtesy of Chicopee Public Library.)

For over 50 years, Chicopee had two separate high schools at Chicopee Center and Chicopee Falls. A new central high school, located on Front Street about halfway between the Falls and the Center, was completed in 1891. An 1890 School Committee report called the central high school "the most important and radical change made in our schools in a generation." (Stawarz Collection; courtesy of Edward Bellamy Memorial Association.)

The new central high school had been open only 25 years when it was destroyed by fire on January 17, 1916. The photograph above dramatically shows the severe weather conditions under which firefighters had to work. (Joseph Morrow Collection; courtesy of Ray Burke.)

For four years, high school classes met at the George S. Taylor School, while a new building was designed and constructed. Some of the area's most prominent architects competed for the project. The design above was submitted by George P.D. Alderman, who had designed Valentine School. Alderman opted for a Classical approach, with an elegant Grecian portico. (Szetela Collection; courtesy of Edward Bellamy Memorial Association.)

The basic shape of the building remained fairly similar for all three designs shown here. They seem to have varied primarily in the amount of ornamentation. Henry Fugere submitted a design that combined the order and symmetry of Classical architecture with subdued Gothic decoration. (Szetela Collection; courtesy of Edward Bellamy Memorial Association.)

For his winning design, Architect George E. Haynes used a style known as Collegiate Gothic, which borrowed elements from Tudor and Gothic architecture. A Boston architect who relocated to Pittsfield, Haynes specialized in school designs. This million-dollar building, which was dedicated in 1920, boasted the first gymnasium in Chicopee's school system. (Courtesy of Edward Bellamy Memorial Association.)

The development of Cabotville Common (shown here around 1900) reflected changing attitudes toward public spaces as Chicopee grew from a town to a city. Cabotville residents first used the land as a common pasture. In 1870, however, the town grew more concerned about appearances. Chicopee passed an ordinance prohibiting "the pasturing or keeping of cattle, goats, or other animals, upon the Common owned by the town." In 1890, the new city went one step further and allocated money to improve the park with walks, benches, and fencing. (Allen/Kerr Collection; courtesy of Edward Bellamy Memorial Association.)

Many of Chicopee's early parks were simply small lots set aside for green space in urban neighborhoods. For example, Bullens Park was originally merchant Isaac Bullens's front lawn. By 1870, the lawn had officially become a park. In 1898, the city decorated the park with an iron fence and a fountain with a statue of a boy holding a swan. By 1936, the Bullens house had been demolished and replaced by a post office. A veterans memorial is now the park's centerpiece. (Lithograph from an ambrotype by D.G. Mason, 1859; courtesy of Edward Bellamy Memorial Association.)

74

By the turn of the century, the city began to see parks, not just as public gardens for people to look at, but as places for citizens to play. Large neighborhood parks like Lincoln Grove in Chicopee Falls began to include baseball diamonds, tennis courts, and playground equipment. In 1910, the city organized a Playground Committee to develop more parks in the city. By 1927, Lincoln Grove was one of six major neighborhood parks. (Courtesy of Chet Kobierski.)

In the 1930s, Chicopee officials began to plan a citywide park that would include playgrounds, picnic areas, woodland, large expanses of open space, and even a pond stocked with game fish. The city designated a large tract of land owned by the Bemis family for park development as part of a WPA project. In 1939, the Bemis tract was dedicated as Szot Park, in memory of Frank Szot, a young Chicopee resident who was killed in WW I. (Szetela Collection; courtesy of Edward Bellamy Memorial Association.)

At first, Chicopee residents had to form their own fire protection associations, because the town as a whole refused to pay for fire apparatus and crews. Chicopee's merchants and industrialists, who had a vested interest in protecting their buildings, played a large part in funding the associations. In 1845, Chicopee Falls organized its first fire district. Three years later, Cabotville followed suit, building a firehouse on land provided by the Cabot Manufacturing Company. In 1873, the Central Fire District bought its first steam fire apparatus. The photograph above, taken in 1874, shows Steam Fire Engine Company #1 posing with their new engine in front of the Atlantic Hall station on Grape Street. In 1893, the city finally authorized funding for a permanent professional fire department. The postcard below shows the Chicopee Falls hose and hook and ladder companies at their station on the corner of Church and Market Streets. (Top: Courtesy of Edward Bellamy Memorial Association—Bottom: Courtesy of Chet Kobierski.)

In 1908, the fire department bought its first motorized apparatus. In the photograph above, members of Hook and Ladder Company #1 show off their new Knox truck in front of the Chicopee Falls Station. The Chicopee Falls station was demolished in 1977, when the new Safety Complex on Church Street was built. (Szetela Collection; courtesy of Edward Bellamy Memorial Association.)

As Chicopee's suburban neighborhoods grew, so did their need for city services. Around the turn of the century, the city constructed many suburban schools, parks, and libraries to accommodate the growing population in outlying neighborhoods. Willimansett's fire station (shown above) was constructed in 1897 as an all-purpose public building, housing the fire department, school offices, and the neighborhood's branch library. (Courtesy of Edwin M. Pajak.)

Chicopee's evolution from settlement to town to city has given it a variety of occasions for celebration. In the photograph at left, citizens celebrate the 300th anniversary of Chicopee's settlement in a 1938 parade through Market Square (actually, celebrants should have waited about 20 years for their parade—the 1638 date is probably erroneous). In the view above, a 1915 parade commemorates the 25th anniversary of the city's charter. (Top: Joseph Morrow Collection; courtesy of Edward Bellamy Memorial Association—Left: Courtesy of Chet Kobierski.)

Chapter Four

A TALE OF TWO TOWNS

Chicopee's early-19th-century growth spurt involved two distinct sites along the Chicopee River where industrial developers could dam the river to run their factories. Chicopee Center and Chicopee Falls became twin communities which are sometimes difficult to tell apart if one takes a quick glance at 19th-century views. The similarity isn't surprising; the industrial centers of both areas were laid out by John Chase and constructed by mason Charles McClallan. McClallan easily adapted his Chicopee Falls designs for construction in Cabotville. During the 1820s and 1830s, many streets in the two villages even had the same names. Each neighborhood quickly developed its own business district, social organizations, and churches. By the 1850s, Chicopee Falls and Cabotville were thriving communities with distinct identities.

The fortunes of the Center and the Falls rose and fell in tandem with their industrial base. Wartime production brought prosperity, while depression hit the villages' industrial workers hard. Both neighborhoods struggled through the 1930s, as industries closed or relocated. World War II brought an economic resurgence that lasted through the 1950s. The 1950s, however, also brought increased mobility, which led to the rapid development of suburban homes, shopping centers, and industries. These changes affected the Center and the Falls in different ways.

Demands for improved transportation and highway construction brought Interstate 91 sweeping through Chicopee Center, cutting off a corner of the village and tempting customers away from the Center's businesses. Route 391 chopped yet another chunk out of the Center. The core of Chicopee Center's business and industrial district remained fairly intact, however. Many of the views of Chicopee Center shown in this chapter are still recognizable today.

Chicopee Falls was a different story. The 1960s were marked by a national drive to eliminate blight and urban decay with a sweep of the bulldozer. Cities received urban renewal funds to tear down whole neighborhoods of neglected old buildings and replace them with modern ones, with no provisions made for renovating and reusing the old. In the 1970s, urban renewal ripped through the heart of Chicopee Falls. By 1980, most of the Chicopee Falls streetscapes shown in this chapter had disappeared.

In this 1856 panorama of Chicopee Center, the village's industrial blocks predominate. To the left of the covered bridge is the Ames Manufacturing Company. To the right are the massive blocks of the Dwight Manufacturing Company. Market Square is visible at the center, just to the left of the smokestack. ("Chicopee, Mass., 1856," lithograph by Endicott & Co., from an ambrotype by Spooner Brothers; Joseph Morrow Collection; courtesy of Ray Burke.)

A viewer has to look carefully at this 1857 lithograph of Chicopee Falls to see the differences between this village and Chicopee Center. The dam and covered bridge are at the far left. The factory immediately to the right of the bridge is Whittemore, Belcher & Co. Next on the right is the Massachusetts Arms Company. The largest mill complex (directly in front of the boys in the foreground) is the Chicopee Manufacturing Company. ("Chicopee Falls 1857," lithograph by Endicott & Co., from an ambrotype by A.F. Daniels; courtesy of Edward Bellamy Memorial Association.)

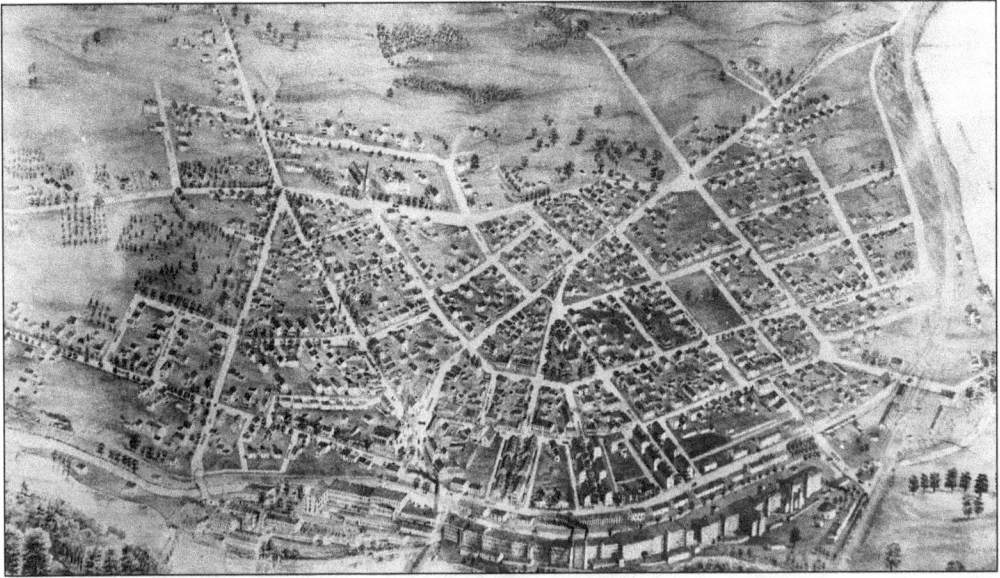

Twenty years later, both the Center and the Falls had become dense urban neighborhoods. These 1878 bird's-eye views show each village's layout. (Chicopee Center is at the top; Chicopee Falls is at the bottom.) Notice the rows of mill buildings arranged like massive brick walls along the river. Behind the mills are the boardinghouses for mill operatives. Commercial buildings then extend out from the industrial core. Next are modest brick and wood-frame buildings crowded together on small lots; these are the homes of shop workers and skilled factory hands—foremen and machinists and overseers. Finally, the larger houses owned by manufacturers, merchants, and professionals are set on large lots overlooking the rest of the village. Even though the two town centers are densely settled, notice how abruptly development stops within about half a mile of the river. At the top of each map, large expanses of open land are still undeveloped and used for farming. (D. Bremer & Co. lithographs of Chicopee and Chicopee Falls, 1878; Top: Joseph Morrow Collection; courtesy of Ray Burke—Bottom: Courtesy of Attorney Francis J. Shea.)

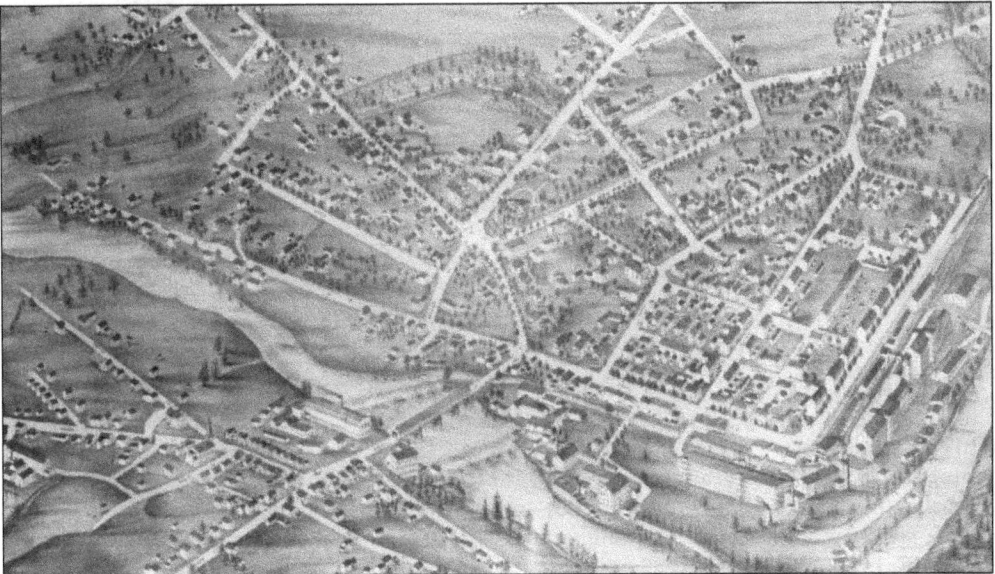

This view of West Main Street in Chicopee Falls, taken during the 1950s, shows the rows of brick boardinghouses that mason Charles McClallan built to house the Chicopee Manufacturing Company's mill workers. (Courtesy of Chicopee Public Library.)

This postcard shows a view of West Main Street looking east some time before 1910. The Hotel DeGray is the building on the right, just behind the horse and carriage. A mixture of early 19th-century wooden residential and business buildings at the western end of the street gave way to larger brick commercial buildings as one traveled east up the street. (Courtesy of Chet Kobierski.)

This view of West Main Street and Broadway in the 1920s shows an active business district lined with brick buildings full of shops, offices, and apartments. The building to the far right is the Father Matthew Total Abstinence Society, built in 1901. Founded in 1869, the society sponsored athletic teams, dramatic societies, parties, and dances—all alcohol-free. The society's facilities included a bowling alley, meeting rooms, a billiard room, and parlors for social gatherings. (Courtesy of Chet Kobierski.)

This 1936 photograph shows the view looking north across the Chicopee Falls bridge. The Father Matthew Total Abstinence Society is to the left. Beyond it is the Lamb Knitting Machine Corporation. This view clearly shows the divided roadway on the 1905 bridge, with separate travel areas for trolleys, automobiles, and pedestrians. (Courtesy of Holyoke Public Library.)

This series of views of the Chapin House on the corner of Church and Main Streets illustrates the successive uses a building might go through over the course of a hundred years. Built in 1834 by Elihu Adams, the Chapin House was one of Chicopee Falls' earliest hotels. By 1875, it had become Wilde's Hotel. Joseph DeGray bought it in the 1890s, renovated the building, and rechristened it the Hotel DeGray. DeGray built an addition to the hotel, creating the city's first theater, the City Opera House (later renamed the DeGray Opera House). The rejuvenated Hotel DeGray is shown below on a festive occasion, probably some time between 1901 and 1911. Besides the opera house, the Hotel DeGray boasted telephone service and its own barbershop. In 1911, DeGray's Opera House became the Grand Theater. (Top: Joseph Morrow Collection; courtesy of Ray Burke—Bottom: Courtesy of Chet Kobierski.)

The top photograph, taken in the 1890s, shows the interior of Joseph R. Beaudoin's barber shop, which was a fixture in the Hotel DeGray from 1894 until 1911. Joseph Beaudoin is the gentleman in the left foreground (the others are unidentified). By 1913, the Hotel DeGray had become the Falls Inn, and lasted for another 24 years under that name. By 1942, the building's ground floor was vacant and the Falls Inn had moved across Church Street to another building. By the time the photograph below was taken (probably in the late 1940s or early 1950s), the Hotel DeGray had become an appliance store. (Top: Szetela Collection; courtesy of Edward Bellamy Memorial Association—Bottom: Courtesy of Albert H. Roy.)

The photographs on these two pages show just a few of the many businesses that prospered in Chicopee Falls. The Union Block at 76 Market Street (shown above) was a meeting place for the Saint Michael's Club, a Polish social organization. To the left of the Union Block is the Langlois Block, where Lawrence Wolfson ran a grocery store from 1934 to 1944, when this photograph was taken. (Photograph by Fonfara Studio; Szetela Collection; courtesy of Edward Bellamy Memorial Association.)

During the 1920s and 1930s, it seemed as though every Chicopee neighborhood had its own movie theater. Willimansett had the Willow; Aldenville had the Midway; Chicopee Center had the Elms (later the Rivoli), the Exchange, the Casino, the Pastime, and the Victoria. Chicopee Falls had the Grand (at the old Hotel DeGray), the Wernick, and the Royal Theater (shown at left), which operated at 139 Main Street from 1917 to 1930. (Hanifan Collection; courtesy of Edward Bellamy Memorial Association.)

The Tivoli, at 9–11 Grove Street, was a popular Chicopee Falls gathering place. William H. Roberts first operated a tavern here in 1905. The photograph above was probably taken in the 1910s, before Prohibition. (The man on the far right is Walenty Konicki; the others are unidentified.) The business operated as a restaurant until 1924, and for a short time was a grocery store. With the repeal of Prohibition, the building once again became a tavern and restaurant, until urban renewal closed it in the 1970s. (Courtesy of Chet Kobierski.)

Although the city was developing rapidly during the 1920s, Chicopee still retained enough farmland to keep the Chicopee Falls Grain Company (at 86 Market Street) in business until 1939. In this 1929 photograph, workers prepare a truckload of feed for delivery. (Hanifan Collection; courtesy of Edward Bellamy Memorial Association.)

One of Chicopee's most famous residents hailed from Chicopee Falls. Born in 1850, Edward Bellamy started his literary career as a journalist for the *New York Evening Post*. He returned to Chicopee, where he became an editor of the *Springfield Union*. With his brother Charles, Bellamy founded the *Springfield Daily News* in 1880. Edward Bellamy is best known for his utopian novel *Looking Backward*, which brought him international fame. (DiCarlo Collection; courtesy of Chicopee Historical Society.)

In 1822, the Second Congregational Church of Chicopee was formed (originally known as the Fifth Congregational Church of Springfield), meeting first at the Belcher family home, and later using a room in one of the Ames Company's buildings. The congregation built its first church in 1833 (it is shown at right in the late 19th century). The spire was added in 1859. This church was demolished during urban renewal in 1970. (Courtesy of Attorney Francis J. Shea.)

88

Not far beyond Chicopee Falls' mills and businesses, open land remained available for farming and recreation. Organized around 1890, the Oxford Country Club was one of America's oldest golf courses. This photograph, taken around the 1940s, shows members posing in front of the clubhouse. Club professional Ed Rubis is on the far right; Frederick Cienciwa Sr. is one of the two caddies leaning against the building in the background. (Courtesy of Chicopee Public Library; gift of Marie and Rick Cienciwa.)

While the core of Chicopee Falls was thickly settled by 1900, one didn't have to go very far from West Main Street to find large tracts of farmland. This view shows Miller's stock farm on Carew Street in the Skipmunk area around 1900. It wasn't long, however, before development moved further out from Chicopee Falls. By 1912, builders were subdividing farms in Skipmunk for house lots. (George Loomis Album; courtesy of Edward Bellamy Memorial Association.)

The heart of Chicopee Center is Market Square, where four major thoroughfares come together. The photograph above provides a bird's-eye view of the square, which is dominated by City Hall. In the foreground is the Robinson train station. Cabotville got its first train station when the Connecticut River Railroad opened a branch through Chicopee in 1845. To the right is the Cabot House. The view below, taken some time between 1870 and 1878, takes a closer look at the Cabot House and the Kendall Block, part of an area of Cabotville called "Merchants' Row." The Cabot House, built in 1834–35, was Cabotville's first hotel. The Kendall Block, also known as the Market Square Hotel, was built in the early 1870s. For a short time, Edward M. Alden ran a bookstore here. Two fires greatly altered Merchants' Row. In the early 20th century, the Cabot House's gable roof was destroyed. In 1976, the Kendall Block lost its upper two stories to a fire. (Joseph Morrow Collection; courtesy of Ray Burke.)

Edward M. Alden's stay in Market Square was short-lived. He went on to become a real-estate developer, subdividing large tracts of land in Chicopee and Holyoke. His son, Percy M. Alden, eventually started his own business in the Kendall Block, the same building where Edward had briefly run a bookstore. From 1915 to 1924, Percy sold bicycles, sporting goods, real estate, auto supplies, paint, and wallpaper from his store in Merchants' Row. Here, Percy poses in front of his shop. (Courtesy of Albert H. Roy.)

The photograph above shows the north side of Exchange Street in the 1890s. The building on the right stands where the Starzyk building is today. Originally known as the Cabot Hall Block, during the 1890s it was occupied by the Wells Opera House and the Chicopee National Bank. The horse-drawn wagon in the middle of the street appears to be carrying a banner advertising Victor bicycles. (Stawarz Collection; Edward Bellamy Memorial Association.)

These two lithographs show Exchange Street in 1859. At the top is the Union Block, on the corner of Exchange and Cabot Streets. Masonic Hall (below) was built in 1848 on the corner of Exchange and Center Streets. The Union Block and Masonic Hall are two of Chicopee's oldest surviving commercial buildings. A list of the buildings' tenants in 1859 illustrates the variety of business services available in the new town. The Union Block housed daguerreotypist and ambrotypist A.E. Alden (Alden made the two ambrotypes from which this lithograph was made), jeweler Theo. F. Morgan, druggist and grocer C.F. Kent, dentist Ralph Morgan, dry goods and millinery dealer Horatio Rice Jr., and boot and shoe dealer D.F. Kendall. Tenants in Masonic Hall included grocers John B. Wood and Warren Smith, merchant tailors L.L. Simmonds and Buckingham & Taylor, and boot and shoe dealer G.H. Chapman. (Lithographs from ambrotypes by A.E. Alden, 1859; courtesy of Edward Bellamy Memorial Association.)

Masonic Hall hadn't changed much by the time this parade marched through Chicopee Center some time between 1936 and 1942. The hall had acquired a new neighbor in the Starzyk Block, built on the other side of Exchange Street in 1920 (occupied by W.T. Grant Co. in the view above). The small wooden building next to Masonic Hall was occupied by the Great Atlantic & Pacific Tea Company, one of the country's earliest supermarket chains. (Courtesy of Mr. and Mrs. Gerard O. LeBlanc.)

This photograph, taken between 1917 and 1920, shows Center Street looking south from Market Square. The Market Square building still stands today, occupied by Wickles Printing. At the far right is the original home of Paul Starzyk's clothing store, which opened in 1917 at 32 Center Street, and was advertised as a "head-to-foot outfitter," "the house that satisfies." Starzyk's business grew so rapidly that he was able to move into a new building in Market Square in 1920. (Courtesy of Edward Bellamy Memorial Association.)

The Universalist church at Market Square, built in 1836, was a unique mixture of sacred and secular spaces. Originally built by the Mechanics' Association for the Universalists, the church was bought by a Presbyterian congregation in 1897. By the time the picture on the left was taken in 1912, Carter & Spaulding's grocery store occupied the ground floor. The photo below shows the proprietors, Joseph Carter (far left) and Justin Spaulding (standing on Carter's right) in front of their store, which they ran from the 1870s until 1914. In 1925, the Presbyterian congregation moved to new quarters on Newbury Street. For a good part of the mid-20th century, the former meetinghouse was home to the Peter Pan café and ballroom, its facade lit by an eye-catching neon sign depicting Peter Pan flying off to Never-Never Land. (Top: Courtesy of Chet Kobierski—Bottom: Courtesy of College of Our Lady of the Elms Archives.)

In this 1931 photograph of Front Street, the automobile has displaced the railroad and is on the verge of replacing the trolley. The old Robinson railroad station closed in 1926. For a few years it served as city offices. By the time this picture was taken, Berestka Motor Sales had taken over the building for its automobile sales showroom. Next to the old station is the Embassy diner, which operated at this site from 1928 to 1978. (Stawarz Collection; courtesy of Edward Bellamy Memorial Association.)

This photograph shows the view looking north along Springfield Street toward Front Street, around 1921. The row houses in the foreground were built as homes for mill workers in the 1830s and 1840s. Before they saw their 100th birthday, the buildings were replaced by the Exchange Building (built in 1928), which now houses the Rivoli Theater. Between City Hall and the row houses, the front of the Chicopee Public Library is visible. (Photograph by Russell Gilbert; courtesy of Chicopee Public Library.)

Chicopee Center had a number of Protestant churches. In 1834, a Congregational society began meeting in Cabotville. When Springfield and Chicopee separated, this church became the Third Congregational Church of Chicopee. This lithograph shows the church's first building at the corner of Springfield and Pearl Streets. ("Chicopee, Mass., 1856," lithograph by Endicott & Co., from an ambrotype by Spooner Brothers; Chicopee Historical Society Collection; gift of Martha L. Doyle and Maxine M. Metras.)

The Unitarian Society was formed in 1841 and held its first meetings at the Cabot Manufacturing Company. Its first church was built at the corner of Cabot and Dwight Streets in 1842. When the city bought that site for the construction of a new fire station in 1893, the congregation built this Shingle Style church at the corner of Fairview Avenue and Grape Street. This church, which featured Tiffany stained-glass windows donated by former Governor George Robinson, was demolished in 1973. (Courtesy of Chet Kobierski.)

Grace Episcopal Church was established in 1846, meeting at first on Cabot Street in a building constructed in 1848. After several false starts, the parish developed a firm footing under the leadership of the Reverend Newton Black in the 1880s. The present church (shown above), built on the corner of Springfield and Pleasant Streets in 1898, was designed by architect Edwin Parlett, who also assisted in designing the Chicopee Public Library. (Courtesy of Chet Kobierski.)

In 1838, a Methodist Episcopal congregation formed in Chicopee Center. They first met on Perkins Street in 1838. They built this elaborate Victorian Gothic church on Center Street in 1884. In 1925, the congregation merged with the Third Congregational Church to form the Federated Church. The church sold its building to the Saint John's Lodge of the International Order of Odd Fellows in 1930. (Courtesy of Chet Kobierski.)

Chicopee Center was such a busy industrial area that it boasted not one, but two railroad depots. Chicopee Junction was built as a Connecticut River Railroad freight depot when the rail line came through Cabotville in 1845. The Chicopee House, shown in the 1859 view above, was built in 1841 by Abner B. Abbey, who developed a number of Chicopee Center streets near this depot. The hotel was moved in 1845 to accommodate the new rail line. The grade crossing, shown below in an 1890s view, was abolished in 1896. (Top: Lithograph from a sketch by E.C. Smith, 1859; courtesy of Edward Bellamy Memorial Association—Bottom: Courtesy of Edward Bellamy Memorial Association.)

Five

TROLLEYS AND PLANES AND AUTOMOBILES

For the first three-quarters of the 19th century, Chicopee's growth was concentrated in Cabotville and Chicopee Falls. Because most working-class people traveled on foot, the locations of businesses and residences were limited by how far someone could easily walk to reach a store or get to work. Since most of the jobs were in the mills, which needed to be near a source of waterpower, development outside of the Center and the Falls was limited to scattered farms and shops. The introduction of the horsecar in the late 19th century removed those limitations, allowing citizens to live farther from their jobs, and allowing businesses to attract customers from outside the immediate neighborhood. The electric trolley and the automobile further increased Chicopee residents' mobility.

In the 1890s, changes in transportation led to the growth of three sections of Chicopee—Willimansett in the northwest, Aldenville in the center, and Fairview in the north. Smart developers bought large tracts of farmland to subdivide into house lots. Residents in these neighborhoods could easily jump on a trolley to head to work, not just in the Falls or the Center, but in Holyoke, South Hadley, or even Springfield. Soon, the new neighborhoods had their own schools, churches, parks, and fire stations. By the 1920s, all three even had their own business districts. The neighborhoods became like towns-within-a-town, each with its own distinct identity.

As the 20th century progressed, and industries no longer needed waterpower to run their machines, some, like A.G. Spalding and the Lamb Knitting Machine Company, moved out to the suburbs to build modern facilities. The three neighborhoods also attracted new manufacturers looking for cheap open land with room for future expansion.

During the late 1930s, growing tensions in Europe brought another major change to Chicopee. The threatening war caused the federal government to re-evaluate its military facilities and look for sites for new military bases. On Chicopee's eastern boundary, a broad plain known as the "tobacco flats" seemed like the perfect site for an Air Force base. After strong lobbying from city officials, the war department chose the Chicopee site. The base brought thousands of new residents, creating demands for new housing, businesses, and public services almost overnight. Although the base was partially closed in 1973, it remains a Reserve base. Many of the base's surplus lands and buildings have been reused for business, housing, and industry.

Chicopee Street, which runs along the Connecticut River north through Willimansett to South Hadley, was one of Chicopee's earliest major roads. Taverns like the 1785 Colonel Abel Chapin stage tavern (shown in a postcard view above) provided food and lodging for travelers passing through Willimansett on foot or horseback. The Chapin tavern was conveniently located near the ferry landing, providing a place for stagecoaches to stop before crossing the river or heading farther north. (Courtesy of Chet Kobierski.)

The lack of a bridge across the Connecticut River into Holyoke delayed Willimansett's development. When the O'Neill family built their house on Erline Street in 1888 (shown in a c. 1891 photograph above), they had to ferry their building supplies across the river from Holyoke. Transportation difficulties meant that Willimansett residents couldn't easily commute to jobs in Holyoke or Chicopee Center. Until the 1890s, farming was the principal occupation for Willimansett residents. (Courtesy of Mr. and Mrs. J.W. Heron.)

In 1842, the Connecticut River Railroad ran its line from Chicopee Junction north through Willimansett and across the river into Holyoke. For 50 years, the railroad bridge and the ferry were the only means of crossing from Willimansett to Holyoke. Willimansett had its own depot (shown in the photograph above) just east of the bridge. While the railroad trestle included a pedestrian walkway, wagons still had to cross the river by ferry for another 50 years. (Courtesy of Chet Kobierski.)

After much wrangling between Chicopee and Holyoke residents, Willimansett finally got its bridge across the Connecticut River in 1893. By 1895, trolleys were making the crossing into Holyoke (the above photograph shows a trolley on the Willimansett bridge in the 1930s). Builders soon began constructing apartment blocks and houses not far from the new bridge. By 1915, Willimansett had become an urban town center with its own businesses. (Courtesy of Holyoke Public Library.)

The McKinstry family can trace its history back to Willimansett's earliest settlement. John McKinstry was the first minister at Chicopee Street's First Congregational Church in 1751. McKinstry Street, which leads from Willimansett east into Aldenville, was named for the McKinstrys whose land it crossed. In this c. 1919 photograph, Willard and Winthrop McKinstry pose with their family produce wagon. Winthrop (standing next to wagon) became known as a Chicopee historian. (Courtesy of the McKinstry Family.)

As Willimansett grew, farms began to give way to subdivisions, apartment buildings, and business blocks. Joseph Tremblay ran a Prospect Street blacksmith shop that had been established by Adjuteur Tremblay in 1898. Craftsmen like Joseph (shown here around 1910 with his sons Fred [left] and Ed [right]), who depended on horses for part of their trade, had to either adapt to the changing neighborhood or go out of business. (Courtesy of the Warren Tremblay Family.)

Because Chicopee Street was one of Chicopee's earliest roads, Chicopee built its first school there around 1715. Through the 1700s and early 1800s, Chicopee Street acquired several schools. As the neighborhood grew, its early schools became inadequate. Perkins School (shown above) was built in 1879 and enlarged in 1888. When the new bridge opened in 1893, Willimansett quickly outgrew the newly enlarged school. In 1898, yet another school (the Chapin School) had to be added to Chicopee Street. (Courtesy of Chet Kobierski.)

Willimansett's growth demanded new churches as well as new schools. In 1888, Willimansett's Protestant community dedicated Beulah Chapel, Chicopee Street's first new church since the construction of the First Congregational Church in 1826. (Photograph by Russell Gilbert, c. 1921; courtesy of Chicopee Public Library.)

In the 1870s and 1880s, real estate developer Edward M. Alden bought 600 acres of land just east of Willimansett. A Ludlow native, Alden had worked for the railroad, the newspaper, and even the pony express before turning to real estate. Alden's office at 602 Grattan Street is shown in the photograph above. Planning to build "a little city on the hill," Alden divided his Chicopee land into building lots, dubbed the area "Aldenville" after himself, and set about creating a mini-land rush. After 1899, when streetcar lines began to link Aldenville, Holyoke, and Chicopee Falls, Alden offered free trolley rides to bring prospective buyers onto the site, enticing them with promises of gifts and prizes to go along with their purchases. He advertised in French and English to attract French-Canadian factory workers from the Falls and the Center to Aldenville. In the photograph below, a trolley packed with potential buyers heads toward the "Grand Auction Sale of Building Lots." (Courtesy of Albert H. Roy.)

"Why be a slave to your landlord?" Alden's ads proclaimed, "when for a few dollars, so to speak, you can have your own happy home?" Aldenville was promoted as "an ideal place to live...on line of Electric Cars, City Water, Parks, and a Catholic church but a step away." Alden's advertisements were so effective that buyers often camped out in order to claim the choicest lots. In the above photo, a tent city of buyers get ready to stake their claims. (Courtesy of Albert H. Roy.)

The new community quickly needed its own school. The four-room wooden school with twin fanlights shown above was built on the corner of McKinstry Avenue and Grattan Street by Marcellin Croteau in 1897. The school is shown here some time before it was expanded in 1907. For a short time during its early history, the school also served as the headquarters for the Aldenville Fire Department. The school was demolished in 1964, and the site is now occupied by Aldenville Common. (Courtesy of Lucky Strike Restaurant, Inc.)

Grattan Street became Aldenville's Main Street. By the early 1900s, it was lined with late Victorian homes (see photograph above). With the installation of the trolley tracks in 1899, the neighborhood expanded rapidly. The trolley meant that workers weren't limited to seeking jobs in their immediate neighborhood. They could live in Aldenville and commute to work in the Center or the Falls or even out of town. Many Aldenville residents commuted to Holyoke rather than to Chicopee businesses or factories. Grattan Street soon became a business center. Stores, restaurants, and offices were clustered near the intersection of Grattan Street and McKinstry Avenue. In the photograph below, Gerry Lamothe and Paul Label stand outside Lamothe's Drug Store, which served Aldenville's residents at 695 Grattan Street from 1919 to 1934. (Notice the sign in the window informing customers the store is closed on Good Friday.) (Top: Courtesy of Albert H. Roy—Bottom: Courtesy of Lucky Strike Restaurant, Inc.)

French-Canadian carpenter Marcellin Croteau built Aldenville's first house on the corner of Grattan and Mary Streets in 1891. He built over 30 houses, as well as several stores, the neighborhood's first school, and its first church. Croteau saw Aldenville grow from scattered farm lots to the busy town shown in the 1953 photograph below. By the 1930s, Aldenville residents had forsaken public transportation for automobiles. In the 1936 photograph at right, Croteau watches the removal of the trolley tracks that had brought the neighborhood's first residents. Compare the 1953 view of Grattan Street below with the c. 1900 photograph on the previous page. Cars have replaced the trolleys. Businesses like the Royal Cafe and the Lucky Strike Restaurant line the western side of the street, forming a mini-business district. In its heyday, Aldenville had its own movie theater, athletic teams, clubs, and even two hospitals. (Top: Courtesy of the Croteau Family— Bottom: Courtesy of Robert Goyette.)

Chicopee's northernmost suburb was originally called "Plainville" because it was situated on a broad flat plain that overlooked Willimansett, Holyoke, and South Hadley. Residents rechristened the neighborhood "Fairview" because it was Chicopee's highest point and commanded an excellent view of the surrounding area. This photograph looking down on North Chicopee from Fairview shows that view around the turn of the century. (Courtesy of Yvette Ducharme.)

This c. 1880 photograph of the Stone farm on Prospect Street shows one of Fairview's earliest farms. James Otis Stone and Maryetta Stone pose in front of the house with their daughter Elsie. The Stone family cultivated over 125 acres on land that is now covered by Memorial Drive. Like Willimansett and Aldenville, Fairview would soon see its farmland replaced with subdivisions and businesses. (Ruby Stone Collection; courtesy of Ray Burke.)

Fairview was the last of Chicopee's major suburbs to be developed. This panorama shows the open agricultural landscape of Fairview around 1920. On the right is Faith Methodist Church, built in 1893. For many years, Faith Methodist was the only Protestant church in Fairview. The building shown above was replaced by the current church in 1930. (Courtesy of Ray Burke.)

Beaudry's Corner, at the intersection of Montcalm and Britton Streets, was a popular Fairview gathering spot. A.J. Beaudry's grocery store was established by Hormisdas Beaudry in 1908, and continued in business until 1954. This view illustrates the changes in transportation that Chicopee was experiencing in the 1920s, as trolleys began to give way to automobiles. Notice the trolley tracks running in front of the building, and the Socony gas pump to the right of the store. (Courtesy of Albert H. Roy.)

Robert's Pond was an important landmark in Fairview. It was not only a place for recreation, but also an economic resource. In the 1913 photograph at left, Henry and Merton Reed cut blocks of ice. The ice was hauled up the chute shown in the photograph below, and packed in sawdust or straw for sale throughout the year. A customer would place a placard in her window to let the iceman know how much ice she needed delivered. (Courtesy of Frances (Reed) Shaw.)

The Smith Highlands neighborhood, where Fairview and Willimansett meet, is named for Quartus Smith, who owned a large tract of land there. The Smith Highlands School was built in 1903, and survived until the 1970s. It is shown here in a c. 1921 photograph by Russell Gilbert. (Russell Gilbert Collection; courtesy of Chicopee Public Library.)

The Montcalm Street School, shown here, was built in 1889 as one of Fairview's neighborhood schools. Originally a two-room schoolhouse, it had been expanded by the time Russell Gilbert took this picture around 1921. Fire destroyed the school in 1951. (Russell Gilbert Collection; courtesy of Chicopee Public Library.)

While much of Chicopee's terrain is broken up by steep hills, the eastern part of the city has a broad expanse of flat land. This area was called the "tobacco flats" because of the number of farms raising tobacco on its sandy soils. The Rollin M. Mason farm (shown above around 1900) was one such farm. In the photograph at left, a group of boys plays baseball in the Mason farm's fields. As early as the 1920s, Chicopee resident Anthony Stonina dreamed of replacing the tobacco flat's farms with an airfield. When Stonina became mayor in the 1930s, he was able to realize his dream. As war threatened Europe in 1939, Stonina lobbied the war department to select Chicopee for its northeast air base. The federal government bought nearly 8 square miles of farmland in Chicopee and Ludlow (including Rollin Mason's farm) to create the new base. (Courtesy of the Mason Family.)

The new base was dedicated in April 1940 and named after Major General Oscar Westover, who had helped found the Army Air Corps. Just before the dedication, 1,400 Civilian Conservation Corps and Works Projects Administration workers began clearing the land for construction. Some of the old farmhouses became temporary offices while construction was under way, while construction firms working on the base used some of the old tobacco barns for storage. Construction proceeded quickly, but the base was still unfinished by the time the United States entered WW II in 1941. In the photograph above, the skeleton of a hangar stands silhouetted against the sky. The photograph below shows the site nearing completion, with barracks and hangars in the background. (Massachusetts WPA photographs; courtesy of Edward Bellamy Memorial Association.)

Air crews quickly moved onto the new base, even while the final phases of construction were being completed. This photograph shows the base in the 1940s, after construction was finished. During WW II, Westover served as a training base for more than 2,000 air crews. Bomber crews from Westover flew to Newfoundland and then on to England for their assignments on the European front. (Courtesy of Albert H. Roy.)

After WW II, Westover became a base for the Berlin airlift. Chicopee became the center for "Operation Little Vittles," a civilian offshoot of the airlift. Volunteers packed about 500 pounds of candy a week for delivery to Berlin's children. This photograph shows some of the "Operation Little Vittles" crew. From left to right they are: Fire Chief Ernest LaFlamme, Richard Cournoyer, Eileen Bieda, Raymond Dashner, Joan Gilman, June Nitera, Laura Chopla, Dorothy Kennedy, Joanne Young, Claire Panzer, Col. Joseph E. Barzynski Jr., Mayor Edward O. Bourbeau, Dolores Belcher, Wilfred Thivierge, and Lt. John W. Parish. ("Operation Little Vittles" Scrapbook; Chicopee Public Library Collection; courtesy of United States Air Force.)

Six

COMING TO AMERICA

As Chicopee developed into an industrial community in the 1820s, the area faced a labor shortage. The resident Yankee population couldn't supply all the workers needed to build dams, canals, mills, boardinghouses, and shops. John Chase and Charles McClallan, agents for the Chicopee Manufacturing and Springfield Canal Companies, began recruiting Irish immigrants from New York, Boston, and Canada to work as masons, carpenters, and laborers. In 1848, the Irish potato famine drove thousands of Irish out of their native land, further increasing Chicopee's Irish community. Around the same time, the Yankee farm girls who had been working as mill hands were growing discontented with their work because of longer hours, higher quotas, and lower wages. Manufacturers found replacements in the town's new Irish residents, who formed ethnic enclaves in Cabotville and Chicopee Falls. By 1858, 60 percent of Chicopee's millworkers were of Irish origin.

In 1859, mill agents began recruiting French Canadians to supplement the Irish work force. Like the Irish, the French Canadians had strong roots in the Catholic Church. About 20 years later, the French Canadians were followed by Polish immigrants. These three ethnic groups formed such a substantial part of Chicopee's population that, as early as 1885, 35 percent of Chicopee's residents were of Irish, French-Canadian, or Polish extraction. These three ethnic groups began to transform the city from a predominantly Protestant community to a predominantly Catholic one.

By the early 1900s, Portuguese and Greek workers had also begun to move into Chicopee. Each ethnic group brought its own language, religion, and culture. They founded their own churches and community organizations to meet their spiritual and social needs. Eventually, each group managed to make a place for itself in Chicopee, gaining both economic and political power. The Irish, French-Canadians, and Polish became numerous enough to elect several mayors from among their ranks.

The growth in Chicopee's Catholic community through the 19th century brought the city a new institution in the form of the Elms Academy, a Catholic school for girls and young women. By 1928, the school had evolved into the first Catholic women's college in Western Massachusetts.

Springfield's first Irish-Catholic residents relied on traveling priests to say Mass. In 1838, Cabotville's Irish community formed Springfield's first Catholic parish, building Saint Matthew's Church at the corner of Pleasant and School Streets. The parish quickly outgrew its original home. In 1859, the congregation hired architect Patrick Keeley to design the Holy Name of Jesus Church (shown at left) on the crest of the hill overlooking Cabotville. (Courtesy of Connecticut Valley Historical Museum.)

The Patrick M. Shea family gathers in front of their home at 112 Belcher Street. Patrick was ten years old when his family came to America in 1850; Bridget Hoar, who became Patrick's wife, arrived in 1847. Like many Irish immigrants, the Shea and Hoar families probably came to America to escape Ireland's potato famine. By the time this family portrait was taken in the 1890s, Patrick had worked his way from blacksmith to storekeeper to proprietor of his own mortuary business. The members of the Shea family, from left to right, are as follows: (front row) Cecelia Shea (standing), Catherine Teresa Shea, and Dorothy Shea; (middle row) Joseph Shea (standing), Frank Shea, Bridget Hoar Shea (Mrs. Patrick M. Shea), Mary Rose Shea, William Scanlon, and Michael I. Shea; (back row) Patrick Shea, Patrick Maurice Shea, and Elizabeth Shea Scanlon. (DiCarlo Collection; courtesy of Chicopee Historical Society.)

Cabotville and Chicopee Falls each had its own Irish community. While Cabotville's Irish residents worshipped at Holy Name, those in the Falls organized their own parish in 1872. They built the first Saint Patrick's Church (shown above in a postcard view) on the north side of the river in 1879. The church was replaced by the present Saint Patrick's in 1948. (Courtesy of Chet Kobierski.)

Not all of Chicopee's Irish immigrants were Catholic. A number were Protestants who moved to Chicopee from Northern Ireland. The photograph above shows Chicopee's North of Ireland band around 1890. The musician behind the big drum on the far right is Robert Burke; the third man to the left of Robert is Robert's brother David. (Courtesy of Ray Burke.)

In the 1860s, French Canadians began to move into Chicopee to work in the town's mills and shops. While at first they worshipped at Holy Name Church, language and cultural differences between Chicopee's Irish and French-Canadian communities caused the French to establish their own parish. The first Assumption church was built on Academy Street in 1874. In 1885, the Victorian Gothic church shown above replaced the first church (Father Bonneville, the parish's founder, is the priest shown in the insert). A fire destroyed the church in 1911. Parishioners worshipped at the L'Union Canadien Hall on Center Street until the present church on Springfield Street was completed in 1925. Churches played a social and cultural role as well as a spiritual one, sponsoring athletic, musical, and theatrical groups. The photograph below shows the Assumption Drum Corps (founded in 1904) gathered in front of the church rectory. (Courtesy of Edward Bellamy Memorial Association.)

Chicopee Falls had its own French-Canadian community. At first they worshipped at Assumption Church. By 1893, however, they had established their own congregation at Saint Joachim's, shown above. In 1923, just a few years after Russell Gilbert took this picture, the present Saint George's Church replaced Saint Joachim's. (Russell Gilbert Collection, c. 1921; courtesy of Chicopee Public Library.)

After the completion of the Willimansett-Holyoke bridge in 1893, Willimansett's population grew quickly. A number of French Canadians settled there, commuting across the bridge to work in Holyoke. By 1897, this new community had built its own church, the Church of the Nativity of the Blessed Virgin Mary (shown at right), at the corner of Chicopee and Newton Streets. In 1979, the old church was torn down when Interstate 391 was built. (Photograph by Russell Gilbert, c. 1921; courtesy of Chicopee Public Library.)

In the 1890s, the new community of Aldenville rapidly became a French enclave. It wasn't long before Aldenville had its own church. Saint Rose de Lima began as a mission church of Willimansett's Nativity parish. Saint Rose's first wooden church (above) was built in 1897 by Marcellin Croteau. Saint Rose officially became a separate parish in 1909. The old wooden church was demolished in 1951 to make way for the present Saint Rose de Lima, which was dedicated in 1954. (Courtesy of Albert H. Roy.)

Marcellin and Marie Croteau were typical of Chicopee's French-Canadian residents, most of whom moved to Chicopee to work in the mills or find jobs in the building trades. The Croteaus settled briefly in Holyoke, where they had this portrait taken. By 1891, they had moved to a new home in Aldenville. A carpenter, Croteau built Aldenville's first church and school, along with dozens of Aldenville's homes and businesses. (Photograph by Demers & Son, Holyoke; courtesy of the Croteau Family.)

Local legend has it that around 1880 a group of Polish immigrants found themselves stranded at the Springfield railroad station. Father Patrick Healey, the pastor of Holy Name Church, supposedly took the new arrivals under his wing and found them homes and jobs in Cabotville. The above photograph, taken in the 1890s, depicts a group of newly arrived immigrants gathered in Market Square. Like the French Canadians before them, the Poles first worshipped at Holy Name Church. However, they soon wanted to establish their own parish to hear services in their own language. The Reverend Stanislaw Chalupka came from Webster to help establish Saint Stanislaus parish in 1890. The church, shown below, was dedicated in 1895. The present Saint Stanislaus church replaced the first building in 1908. The old church served as the parish's hall and school until its demolition in 1925. (Top: Stawarz Collection; courtesy of Edward Bellamy Memorial Association—Bottom: Russell Gilbert Collection, c. 1921; courtesy of Chicopee Public Library.)

Like the French and the Irish, Chicopee's Polish settlers quickly established their own religious, social, and athletic organizations. The *c.* 1914 photograph above shows members of a Polish fraternal organization (possibly the Polish lancers) gathering at the corner of School and Dwight Streets in Chicopee Center. (Courtesy of Chet Kobierski.)

In 1897, The Polish National Church, or Holy Mother of the Rosary Church, was constructed for Polish immigrants who followed the Orthodox Catholic rite. Damaged by fire in 1932, the church was rebuilt and rededicated in 1933. It is shown here around 1939. (Photograph by Fonfara Studio; Szetela Collection; courtesy of Edward Bellamy Memorial Association.)

Chicopee's Polish settlers immigrated to find political freedom as well as economic opportunity. Many of them came from Austrian-dominated areas in the south of Poland. In the photograph above, a 1910s parade float depicts "Poland in Present Time." The float appears to portray Poland's oppression by Germany, Russia, and Austria. Chicopee's Polish residents maintained their language and culture by forming a number of social clubs. By 1915, Chicopee's city directory listed at least 20 Polish associations providing social, educational, and financial services. The Polish National Home (the building in the background above) was built in 1912–14 to provide citizenship education for Poles while helping them retain their cultural identity. The Jan Sobieski Club (below) was founded in 1914 to provide insurance for members of the Polish community. (Top: Joseph Morrow Collection; courtesy of Edward Bellamy Memorial Association—Bottom: Photograph by Fonfara Studio; Szetela Collection; courtesy of Edward Bellamy Memorial Association.)

Around 1905, Chicopee began to see its first Greek immigrants. The community grew quickly, forming a Greek Orthodox Society in 1917. The society built its own church in Chicopee Falls in 1920. The original Saints Helen and Constantine Church (shown above around 1921) was replaced by the present church in 1956. (Photograph by Russell Gilbert; courtesy of Chicopee Public Library.)

Chicopee's new Greek residents followed their Irish, French-Canadian, and Polish predecessors to jobs in Chicopee's industries. Many worked at the Dwight mills and the Stevens-Duryea factory. Like the other immigrant groups, the Greeks organized social clubs to help them preserve their culture and language. The photograph above shows members of the Pan-Greek Society participating in a 1921 Memorial Day Parade through Chicopee Center. (Photograph by Russell Gilbert; courtesy of Chicopee Public Library.)

124

In the 1850s, Portuguese immigrants began settling in Massachusetts coastal towns, and working in whaling and fishing communities like New Bedford. By the 1890s, a new wave of Portuguese residents began to find homes farther inland in towns along the Connecticut River. In Chicopee, they followed the example of their Irish, Canadian, and Polish predecessors, and went to work in the mills in the Center and the Falls. Like their predecessors, they maintained their culture and language through church and social groups. The above photograph shows members of the Portuguese-American Club at the club's ground-breaking ceremonies. From left to right are: Father Thomas A. Shea (Holy Name pastor), Mayor Demers, Herman King, Mr. Starczyk, and Edward Chapdelaine. Below, members display the club's banner. From left to right are Antonio Fonseca, Anizo Antonio, Ovido Peres, Antonio Nunes, and Herman King (the young women in the photograph are unidentified). (Photographs by Dick Boisvert; courtesy of the Chicopee Portuguese Club.)

By the late 19th century, immigrants in Chicopee and surrounding towns had formed a sizable Catholic community. Springfield Bishop Thomas Beavens and Sisters of Saint Joseph Mother Superior John Berchmans felt the community needed a Catholic academy for girls and young women. In 1899, the Academy of Our Lady of the Elms opened on Springfield Street (above). The 1900 photograph below shows some of the academy's students. From left to right they are as follows: (front row) Jennie Flanagan, Welthia May Snow, and Jennie Cavanaugh; (second row) Sadie Murphy (Sr. Rose Michael), Kitty Dunne (Sr. M. Carmelite), Angela Marin (Sr. Rose Agnes), Pansie Snow, Miss Healey, and Mary Carlin; (third row) Sadie Kane, Jennie Kelly (Sr. Thomas Daniel), Katherine Keenan (Sr. Margaret Elizabeth), Annie Kelly (Sr. M. Seraphim), Mary Kenny, and Margaret Stanton (Sr. Agnes Cecelia); (back row) Annie Otis, Agnes Neary, Martha Lithcoe (Sr. M. De La Salle), Ada Godfrey, Lucy Joyce (Mrs. Michael Morrissey), Bridget Hussey (Sr. Mary Gualberta), Nora (Honor) Bagley (Sr. M. Marcella), Annie Casey, and Catherine Begley (Sr. M. Hyacinth). (Top: Courtesy of Chet Kobierski—Bottom: Courtesy of College of Our Lady of the Elms Archives.)

From its founding, the Elms was both an academy, offering the equivalent of a high school education, and a normal school, offering college-level courses to prepare students for teaching careers. The photograph above, taken in front of the academy's chapel (built in 1913), illustrates the age range of the academy's pupils, from girls to young women in their early 20s. By the 1920s, Mother Berchmans was working to transform the academy into a college that would provide Catholic women with the same educational opportunities that Holy Cross College provided for young men. Mother Berchmans and Bishop O'Leary began an ambitious building campaign, hiring architect John W. Donohue to design a new residence hall in 1924. The c. 1940s photograph below shows Elms students practicing archery on the lawn near O'Leary Hall. In 1928, the Elms received its charter as a four-year women's college. By 1932, Donohue had added a grand Administration Building to the campus. (Courtesy of College of Our Lady of the Elms Archives.)

BIBLIOGRAPHY

Aherne, Sister Consuelo Maria, S.S.J. *Joyous Service: The History of the Sisters of Saint Joseph of Springfield*. Holyoke, MA: Sisters of Saint Joseph, 1983.

Babbitt, G.H.T. *Chicopee Falls Past and Present*, 1893.

Babcock, Glenn D. *History of the United States Rubber Company: A Case Study in Corporation Management*. Indiana University: Bureau of Business Research, 1966.

Barber, John Warner. *Historical Collection...of Every Town in Massachusetts*. Worcester: Dorr, Howland and Co., 1839.

Edward Bellamy Memorial Association Local History Collections.

Chicopee Municipal Registers, 1848–1965.

Chicopee Public Library Local History Vertical Files.

Everts, Louis H. *History of the Connecticut Valley in Massachusetts, with Illustrations and Biographical Sketches of Some of its Prominent Men and Pioneers*. Philadelphia: J.B. Lippincott & Co., 1879.

Hamilton, John D. *The Ames Sword Company: 1829–1935*. Providence, Rhode Island: Mowbray Co., 1983.

Holland, Josiah Gilbert. *History of Western Massachusetts: The Counties of Hampden, Hampshire,*
  Franklin, and Berkshire. Springfield, Massachusetts: Samuel Bowles & Co., 1855.

Johnson, L.L. *Chicopee Illustrated, 1896*. Holyoke, MA: Transcript Publishing Company, 1896.

Kerr, Bessie Warner. "A History of Chicopee." *The Chicopee Herald*, 1945–46.

McConnell, Sharon, editor. *Chickuppy and Friends*, 1981–87.

McKinney & Smith. *Map of the Villages of Chicopee and Chicopee Falls, Hampden County Massachusetts*. Philadelphia: W.H. Rease's Lithographic Establishment, 1859.

McKinstry, Winthrop. *Glimpses of the Past*. Chicopee, MA: Alice McKinstry Hawes, 1978.

Midura, Gladys. "Saint Stanislaus Bishop and Martyr Parish, 1891–1991: A Century of Faith and Dedication." Typescript, 1991.

Serven, James E. "In Search of the 'Ideal' Rifle." *American Rifleman*, Nov 1969, pp. 52–5.

Shlakman, Vera. *Economic History of A Factory Town: A Study of Chicopee, Massachusetts*. 1935.
  Reprint, New York: Octagon Books, 1969 reprint.

Spence, Vina. "The Manufacturing Industries of the City of Chicopee, Massachusetts." Master's thesis, Clark University, 1930.

Szetela, Thaddeus M. *History of Chicopee*. Chicopee, MA: Szetela & Rich Publishing Company, 1949.

www.ingramcontent.com/pod-product-compliance
Lightning Source LLC
Chambersburg PA
CBHW080854100426
42812CB00007B/2017